Christmas

in

New Mexico

Recipes, Traditions and Folklore
for the Holiday Season

by Lynn Nusom

Author of "New Mexico Cook Book"

GOLDEN WEST ☼ PUBLISHERS

Cover design—*The Book Studio*

Front Cover Photo—Luminarias are lit each Christmas Eve on the plaza in Mesilla, New Mexico. Photo by Russell and Pamela Bamert.

Back cover and other illustrations by Randall Cantrell.

Interior photos by Lynn Nusom, except as otherwise credited.

Other books by Lynn Nusom:

> *New Mexico Cook Book*
> *Christmas in Arizona Cook Book*
> *The Tequila Cook Book*

Library of Congress Cataloging-in-Publication Data
Nusom, Lynn.
Christmas in New Mexico / by Lynn Nusom.
p.   cm.
Includes Index.
1. Christmas Cookery.   2. Cookery—New Mexico
3. Christmas-New Mexico I. Title
TX739.2.C45N87 1991   641.5'68—dc20   91-34113
ISBN 0-914846-59-0   CIP

Golden West Publishers, Inc.
4113 N. Longview Ave.
Phoenix, AZ 85014, USA
(602) 265-4392

Golden West Publishers books are available at special discounts to schools, clubs, organizations and businesses for use as fund-raisers, premiums and special promotions. Send inquiry to Director of Marketing.

Dedication

This book is dedicated with heartfelt thanks to my wife, Guylyn Morris Nusom, a third generation New Mexican, who came up with the original concept of presenting the unique expression of Christmas in New Mexico.

Her assistance with all phases of the preparation of this book, including researching, testing recipes, proofreading, and finding photographic materials, was invaluable.

Acknowledgements

My sincere gratitude to Anita Worthington and Cheryl Thornburg, who contributed their excellent editing prowess to help shape the book, and to the Mesilla Valley Writers Critique Group for all their help and kind encouragement while creating this book.

And a very special thanks to many wonderful New Mexicans who have generously shared their stories and recipes with me.

CONTENTS

Main Dishes

Side Dishes

Chapter Seven, **_Christmas in the Pueblos_** .... **_77_**

Cakes and Pies

Chapter Eight, **_Christmas in the City Different_** ....**_95_**

Christmas Sweets

Chapter Nine, **Christmas in the Duke City** **113**

Fruits and Puddings

Chapter Ten, **The Many Cultures of a New Mexican Christmas ..123**

Beverages

INTRODUCTION

I remember all the Christmases spent in upstate New York, Manhattan, Spain, and Bermuda. But until I moved to New Mexico with my wife, Guylyn, I never realized how different and unique Christmas could be!

Yes, it sometimes snows in New Mexico, and all the merchants start putting up their Christmas decorations around Halloween, and the day after Thanksgiving is the busiest shopping day of the year. But the events leading up to Christmas in New Mexico are indeed rare, wondrous, and truly enchanted!

There are so many memories . . .

The first time I attended the Feast of Guadalupe, which begins the Christmas season on December 12th. . .

Playing in the sand at the White Sands National Monument while the Christmas day sun beat down upon our heads . . .

Roller skating in front of the Baptist church on Christmas Day, and singing "Jingle Bells". . .

Having Christmas dinner in the 50-year-old French colonial home my in-laws built, and watching the snow gently falling in front of the many-paned windows . . .

Waking up on Christmas morn in a centuries-old adobe, and feeling the presence of the New Mexicans who had celebrated Christmas in that house so many years ago. . . .

Embarking on a posada over a crooked road and mistaking a palomino for the guitar player . . .

Walking the streets of Santa Fe, and feeling as if one were in a living creche . . .

Getting the sense of just how magical Christmas in New Mexico is, when the luminarias appear around the tops of adobe buildings just as in territorial days . . .

In this book we share some of these memories and hope
to give you a glimpse of how very, very special
Christmas in New Mexico
really is!

Chapter One

The Feast of Guadalupe

For many New Mexicans, the Christmas season starts on December 12th with the Feast of Our Lady of Guadalupe, the patroness of the Americas. Legend has it that she made her first appearance in Mexico in 1531 to an Indian who had converted to Christianity.

Parishioners believe that Our Lady of Guadalupe enriches their lives, lightens their daily burdens and protects their homes. One can see statues of the saint in many homes in New Mexico. The celebration every December is their way of thanking her for all she does for them throughout the year.

One of the most colorful and active presentations of the Feast of Our Lady of Guadalupe is in Tortugas, just outside of Las Cruces.

Upon learning this, I slung my camera over my shoulder and set out to see the festivities for the first time.

The sky was a sad, unusual gray, and it seemed extremely bleak as I drove up. Soon, however, the brilliant feathers of the Indian dancers and the Sunday-best of the other worshippers lightened my spirits.

Diverse sights and sounds surrounded me. Shy little girls in fancy red velvet dresses with lace collars held hands and giggled. Indians lounged against ancient pickup trucks waiting for the dances to begin. And boastful young men in jeans swaggered about.

As I wandered among the spectators and participants trying to get my light meter to register something, I noticed that the predominant language was Spanish.

I also noticed that there weren't many "outsiders" watching the Indian dancers. I asked a fellow visitor if the low turnout was due to the weather.

"No," he said. "These folks don't do this to attract tourists—they do it for themselves. I think they'd be just as happy if none of <u>us</u> were here."

Just then the drums started, and the Indians began their hypnotic dance, snaking in and out of line down the dirt street.

During a break in the dancing, people drifted to the community hall to eat lunch. The dancers hung their headdresses on tree branches, and kids played around the few booths that had been set up to honor Guadalupe or sell snacks.

Part of the celebration includes a 14-mile pilgrimage to the top of Tortugas Mountain on the evening of December 11th. The faithful carry torches to light the way and gather wood as they go for a bonfire that will light up the dark sky.

Once at the top, they sing and pray until dawn, when they return to the village to continue their worshipful celebration.

The meals served during the Feast of Guadalupe celebration are an extremely important part of the observance.

Pat Beckett, a prominent archaeologist, writer, and bookstore owner, has been in charge of the kitchen in Tortugas for the feast for the past 25 years.

When I talked to Mr. Beckett, he indicated that feeding every-

**Tortugas Indian Headdress
at the
Feast of Guadalupe**

one was a monumental task. An entire steer is donated to the group. The bones are boiled in water to make the broth in which the albondigas (meatballs) are cooked. The meat is ground to make the albondigas and the red chile with meat dish. Thirty or more women roll out the tiny meatballs, which are cooked in the beef broth overnight.

The meal is served after the dances. The dancers eat first; then anyone who comes to the door is fed, as long as the food lasts. They serve between 1,000 and 1,500 people each year. Although there is no cost for the dinner, donations are gratefully accepted.

The menu, since Mr. Beckett has been doing it, is always the same: Macaroni and Cheese, Albondigas, Red Chile with Meat, Beans, and Indian Bread.

Bean Dip Extraordinaire

1/4 cup OLIVE OIL
2 cloves GARLIC, minced
3 or 4 GREEN ONIONS,
    finely chopped
1/2 yellow ONION,
    finely chopped
1 Tbsp. PARSLEY, finely
    chopped
3 cups PINTO BEANS,
    cooked and mashed

1/2 cup plain YOGURT or
    sour cream
1/2 tsp. SALT
1/2 tsp. CUMIN
2 tsp. ground RED CHILE
    POWDER
1 Tbsp. JALAPENOS, chopped
1 cup SWISS CHEESE, grated

Saute garlic, yellow and green onions, and parsley in olive oil until soft. Mix onion mixture with beans, yogurt, cumin, salt, chile powder, and jalapenos. Cook until warmed through. Spoon mixture into a serving bowl or chafing dish. Sprinkle cheese on top and serve warm surrounded by tostados.

Brie Pie

This unusual recipe will have the guests at any party talking.

PUFF PASTRY*
1 5-lb. BRIE CHEESE WHEEL
1 cup APRICOT PRESERVES
1 Tbsp. ORANGE PEEL, grated

1/4 cup BRANDY
1 cup PECANS, chopped
1/4 cup melted BUTTER

Split brie wheel in half, making two equal layers. Mix apricot preserves, orange peel, and brandy together. Spread this mixture on one half of brie. Sprinkle nuts on top and replace other half of the wheel. Wrap puff pastry around brie. Make several holes in the pastry with a fork to allow steam to escape. If you have any pastry left you can make Christmas designs using small cookie cutters and apply to top. Spread with melted butter and bake in a 400 ° oven for 15 to 20 minutes or until pastry is golden brown. Cut wedges and serve with fruit or crackers.

Use your favorite recipe or buy it frozen from a gourmet food shop.

Caviar and Avocado Dip

2 large ripe AVOCADOS
1/2 cup SOUR CREAM
3 Tbsp. LIME JUICE

1/8 tsp. CAYENNE PEPPER
4 Tbsp. BLACK CAVIAR

Mash avocados, and blend in sour cream, lime juice, and cayenne. Mound on a serving plate and make a well in the top. Fill with caviar and serve with Melba rounds or fine crackers.

Chile Cheese Popcorn

8 cups of popped POPCORN
2 Tbsp. BUTTER
1/2 tsp. RED CHILE POWDER

1/2 tsp. GARLIC SALT
1/4 cup PARMESAN CHEESE

Mix together the butter, red chile powder and garlic salt. Pour over popcorn, toss. Sprinkle on the cheese and toss again.

Corn and Red Pepper Relish

1 can (17 oz.) WHOLE KERNEL
     CORN, drained
1 cup RED BELL PEPPER, diced
4 GREEN ONIONS, chopped
1/4 cup TARRAGON VINEGAR
2 Tbsp. OLIVE OIL

1 Tbsp. SUGAR
1 tsp. CELERY SALT
1 CLOVE GARLIC, minced
1/2 tsp. SALT
1/2 tsp. ground RED CHILE
     POWDER

Mix the ingredients together and let chill in the refrigerator for at least 2 hours before serving.

Serves 6 - 8.

Fiery Red Caviar Dip

1 cup SOUR CREAM
1 tsp. LEMON JUICE
1/2 WHITE ONION, finely
    chopped

1 jar (4 oz.) RED CAVIAR
1/4 tsp. CAYENNE PEPPER
several dashes of TABASCO®

Mix all the ingredients together. Chill in the refrigerator for one hour and serve with raw vegetable sticks or crackers.

Green Pepper & Jalapeno Jelly

This is a traditional Christmas gift in New Mexico. One year we had so many jars given to us, we planned a party around it..

2 cups GREEN BELL PEPPERS,
    finely chopped
1/4 cup JALAPENOS, seeded
    and finely chopped
2 cups white VINEGAR

4 cups SUGAR
1 tsp. SALT
1 bottle (6 oz.) LIQUID FRUIT
    PECTIN

Blend bell pepper and jalapenos with vinegar in a blender, a little at a time, until you have a smooth mixture. Put mixture in a saucepan (not aluminum) with sugar and salt. Bring to a boil. Reduce heat and let cook for 10 more minutes. Let cool. Strain through a fine sieve; then stir in pectin.

Pour into 1/2-pint jars, leaving 1/2-inch head space. Process in a hot water bath; let cool and store in the refrigerator.

Yield: 5 or 6 half-pint jelly jars.

Pecan Cheese Ball

**1 8-ounce package CREAM
        CHEESE**
**2 cups CHEDDAR CHEESE,
        grated**
1 cup GREEN CHILE, chopped

1 Tbsp. dry SHERRY WINE
1 Tbsp. PARSLEY, chopped
1 clove GARLIC, minced
1 cup PECANS, finely chopped

Mix together all the ingredients, except pecans, and form into a ball. Chill in the refrigerator for at least 1 hour. Roll the ball in chopped pecans. Serve with your favorite crackers.

Quesadillas

**1 cup MONTEREY JACK
        CHEESE, grated**
4 large FLOUR TORTILLAS
1 tsp. CILANTRO, chopped

JALAPENOS to taste
**1 Tbsp. BLACK OLIVES,
        sliced**
1 Tbsp. PIMENTOS, diced

Divide cheese into fourths and sprinkle over one half of each tortilla. Divide rest of the ingredients into fourths and sprinkle over cheese. Fold tortillas in half over the cheese. Bake in a 350 ° oven for 10 minutes or until cheese melts. Remove from oven and cut tortillas into wedges (3) and serve at once.

Serves 4.

Red Chile Con Queso

We met some folks from the Midwest recently and I started talking about "queso." They looked at me like I'd lost my mind. But here, in New Mexico, we eat chile con queso (melted cheese with green chile in it) and chips all the time. Most folks make it with just green chile, but we like to add some red chile as well to our queso.

2 cups (1 lb.) VELVEETA®
   cheese, cubed
1/4 cup EVAPORATED MILK
1 tsp. GARLIC POWDER
1/2 tsp. OREGANO
1/2 tsp. CUMIN

1/2 tsp. SALT
1/2 ONION, finely chopped
1/2 cup GREEN CHILE,
   chopped
1/2 tsp. RED CHILE POWDER

Melt cheese in a microwave or a saucepan. Stir in remaining ingredients, adding more milk if necessary. Heat again just until warm. Serve with tortilla chips.

Yield: approx. 2 cups.

Salami Horns

1 pkg. (8 oz.) CREAM CHEESE
1/2 cup DATES, chopped
1/2 cup PECANS, chopped
1 Tbsp. BRANDY

1/2 pound HARD SALAMI,
   thinly sliced
PARSLEY, as desired

Mix cream cheese, dates, pecans, and brandy together. Put a tablespoon of this mixture on one edge of each slice of salami and roll salami into a horn shape. Secure salami horn with a frilled toothpick. Place a small piece of parsley into the cream cheese at one end. Arrange horns on a serving plate and serve as hors d'oeuvres.

Salmon Party Ball

1 can (6 1/2 oz.) SALMON,
    drained
1 pkg. (8 oz.) CREAM CHEESE,
    at room temperature
1 Tbsp. LEMON JUICE

1 tsp. HORSERADISH
2 cloves GARLIC, minced
1 Tbsp. PARSLEY, chopped
1/2 cup PECANS, chopped

Combine all ingredients, except pecans. Roll into a ball. Chill in refrigerator until firm. Then roll in the pecans and serve with your favorite crackers.

Señor Pat's Pecan Paté

Pat Healy has lived in New Mexico, at least part of each year, all his life. A great decorator and party giver—he has made many houses, including ours, sparkle with his special touch at Christmas time.

1 cup GREEN BELL PEPPER
1 cup PECANS
liberal dashes of TABASCO®

Grind the bell pepper in a food processor. Add pecans and grind. Add Tabasco and serve with crackers.

Yields approx. 2 cups.

Shrimp Cheese Ball

Another, perhaps common, event in most towns and cities is practiced to a fine art in Santa Fe—and that is a party. Some of the finest soirees we have ever attended have been here. Many hosts and hostesses pay particular attention to the hors d'oeuvres and here are a couple of fine examples.

2 cans (4 1/4 oz.) tiny SHRIMP, drained
1 package (8 oz.) CREAM CHEESE, at room temperature
8 oz. CHEDDAR CHEESE, grated, at room temperature

1 tsp. DILLWEED, chopped
1 tsp. PARSLEY, chopped
1/2 tsp. GARLIC SALT
1/4 tsp. CAYENNE PEPPER
1/2 cup ALMONDS, sliced

Mix all the ingredients together, except almonds. Roll into a ball and chill in the refrigerator until firm. Then roll in the almonds and serve with your favorite crackers.

Sweet Potato Chips

Large SWEET POTATOES
OIL for deep frying
SALT

Peel the potatoes and slice as thinly as possible. Let slices stand in cold water for 2 hours. Dry very well. Fry, a few at a time, in oil heated to 375°, until they are a golden brown. Drain; sprinkle with a little salt and serve.

Chapter Two

Las Posadas

The cherished tradition of the posadas originally began on December 16th and lasted until Christmas Eve. Carved figures of Mary and Joseph were carried through the streets in search of an inn. Each night, the weary travelers were finally given shelter in a home—and then the party began.

Today, celebrants at the posadas often condense the observance into one evening, going from house to house on Christmas Eve. Drinks and Christmas goodies are served at each home they visit. Sometimes carols are sung, with the accompaniment of a guitar, outside their neighbor's door.

The Tradition of the Posada

The December night is cold, and there are snow flurries in the air.

One of the group says, "And everybody thinks it's hot in New Mexico."

Someone else laughs, and they continue on their mission, wrapped up against the chill in the air. They reach an adobe house—hard to tell if it was built 300 years ago or in the last decade. They raise their voices in a familiar Christmas carol.

The words, written centuries ago, are sung in Spanish although now and then a caroler inserts an English word. The verses tell the story of Mary and Joseph pleading for a pallet of hay at the inn only to be turned away.

This ancient ritual is known as Las Posadas meaning "The Inns". It reenacts the couple's search for lodging in Bethlehem the night the Christ child was born.

Many versions of the posadas exist. Traditionally—from December 16th through Christmas Eve, families and friends gather each evening. They may first say a prayer or recite the Rosary. Afterward they form a procession and visit other homes in their neighborhood or community.

Upon reaching their destination, a song frames the plea to gain admittance. The home's occupants open wide their door; urge the visitors to come in, and ply them with refreshments.

This custom is said to have been introduced into New Mexico almost 400 years ago by Fray Diego de Soria, an Augustinian missionary. He wanted a ritual that would counteract those practiced at the time—namely, celebrations in honor of gods of war. He obtained permission from the Vatican to use the idea of St. Ignatius Loyola to say a prayer on nine successive days (a novena) that would recall the journey of Mary and Joseph.

The native Indians of New Mexico loved pageantry as much as the conquering Spaniards. So they readily accepted the Christian stories. Over time the stories were often adapted to particular areas, so we get many different versions of the Posada.

One can only imagine the Indians' bewilderment when the good friars read the biblical passage that sets forth the basis of the posada:

1. *And it came to pass in those days that there went out a decree from Caesar Augustus, that all the world should be taxed.*

2. *(And this taxing was first made when Cyrenius was governor of Syria.)*

3. *And all went to be taxed, every one into his own city.*

4. *And Joseph also went up from Galilee, out of the city of Nazareth, into Judaea, unto the city of David, which is called Bethlehem: (because he was of the house and lineage of David:)*

5. *To be taxed with Mary his espoused wife, being great with child.*

6. *And so it was, that, while they were there, the days were accomplished that she should be delivered.*

7. *And she brought forth her first-born son, and wrapped him in swaddling clothes, and laid him in a manger; because there was not room for them in the inn.*

St. Luke, Chapter II, 1 - 7.

(Above version from ***The Holy Bible*** published by Wanzer, Foote & Co., Rochester, N.Y., 1850. Originally owned by Samuel Blakesley and Rhoda Hayes Nusom, the author's great, great grandparents.)

The lyrics of Las Posadas tell the simple story in song. Shown below is the melody followed by an English translation of the song.

LAS POSADAS

¿ Quién les da - po - sa - da a es - tos pe - re -
gri - nos, que vie - nen can - sa
dos de - an - dar los ca - mi - nos?
Por más que di - gá - is que ve - nís ren -
di - dos, no da - mos po - sa - da
a des - co - no - ci - dos.

(Reprinted from **El Mundo Espanol**. Vol. II, 1942, by permission of D. C. Heath and Company.)

Las Posadas
(English translation)

Saint Joseph: Who will give lodging to these pilgrims, who are tired out from traveling the highways?

Innkeeper: However much you may say that you are worn out, we do not give lodging to strangers.

Saint Joseph: In the name of heaven, I beg of you lodging, since my beloved wife can travel no longer.

Innkeeper: There is no lodging here; keep on moving. I cannot open to you, don't be stupid.

Saint Joseph: Don't be inhuman and have pity, for the God of the Heavens will reward you for it.

Innkeeper: Now you may go away and not bother me, because if I get mad I'm going to beat you.

Saint Joseph: We come worn out from Nazareth; I am a carpenter by the name of Joseph.

Innkeeper: Your name doesn't concern me; let me sleep, since I have already told you that we are not to open to you.

Saint Joseph: Lodging, dear Innkeeper, for only one night, the Queen of the Heavens begs of you.

Innkeeper: Well then if she is a queen who asks it, how is it that at night she goes so unattended?

Saint Joseph: My wife is Mary, the Queen of the Heavens; mother she will be of the Divine Word.

Innkeeper: Is it you, Joseph and your wife Mary? Enter pilgrims; I did not know you.

Saint Joseph: Happy be this house that gives us lodging; may God always give you your sacred happiness.

Innkeeper: Lodging we give you with much happiness; enter, honest Joseph, enter with Mary.

Chorus: (from without), Enter saintly pilgrims; receive this ovation, not from this poor dwelling but from my heart.

Chorus: (from within), This night is (made) of happiness, of pleasure, and of rejoicing, because we give lodging here to the Mother of the Son of God.

Our fondest memories of a posada are of the first Christmas we spent in our old adobe in San Jose, New Mexico. San Jose is a sleepy little town beside the Pecos River. When we lived there, it was inhabited solely by Spanish-speaking Americans of both Spanish and Mexican descent and—ourselves.

The house was a delightful rabbit warren of 11 rooms mostly connected through a central patio. Of course, there was no central heating, and we spent a lot of time feeding a generous supply of wood into the many stoves and fireplaces.

One of the men who renovated our house was a native of San Juan, just across the road from San Jose. He invited us to join him and his family and friends in a posada.

Our small group, including one gentleman with a guitar, stopped at each house and serenaded the residents with Christmas carols in Spanish. We soon caught onto the words and after a couple of stops and with the ingestion of some great home-made wine and a little tequila, we were singing as lustily as everyone else.

Burro Mountain

The following was printed in the **Mesilla News**, La Mesilla, New Mexico on September 1, 1938.

OLD SPANISH CUSTOM, TRANSPLANTED TO NEW SPAIN, FEATURES MEXICAN CELEBRATION OF CHRISTMAS IN LAS CRUCES CATHOLIC CHURCH

An old and quaint custom, preparing for the celebration of Christmas, is being enacted every evening inside and on the grounds of St. Genevieve Church. This is the novena commemorative of the journey of the Blessed Mother and St. Joseph from Nazareth to Bethlehem, or "posadas," as it is popularly known. It is held at seven every evening except Sunday when it will be at three p.m.

The custom of the Novena, or nine days' prayer, is one of the very oldest Christian devotions, beginning with the apostles themselves "preserving in prayer" the nine days between the ascension and pentecost. But from a Spanish custom, transplanted to the new world in the early days, this particular novena has been made more dramatic. Action has been added to prayer and the result is both interesting and devotional.

After a few prayers, the choir sings the thanks of the holy pilgrims for the previous night's lodging and they set forth, typified by statues which are borne on a handbarrow (sic) in procession. In Las Cruces, a figure of a burro taken from the Christmas set is added and also the snowy woods, through which the travelers wend their way.

Preceded by the usual processional cross and the congregation, the barrow is borne around the paths of the church garden, the choir and people meanwhile singing a hymn for the journey (music being a necessity for the better effect of any procession).

On the return to the church the pilgrims find the doors closed against them and considerable argument and explanation is required in songs between those within, representing hard-hearted landlords, and the pilgrims without. The words indicate that they are supposed to be rejected at house after house until finally they convince a more charitable host; the doors are swung wide and the procession enters with songs of joy and thankfulness.

The regular prayers of the novena follow, interspersed with lively hymns of a popular simplicity and vigor; the whole concluding with a hymn of appeal for the coming of the Savior . . .

Altogether it makes a very satisfactory evening; combining prayer, music, drama and recreation, and as such is quite popular. There is nothing rigid about the affair, the hymns being chosen according to the preference of the locality. Some of those sung here are quite modern, other, notably the argument at the door, are of very ancient Spanish style and probably were brought over by early missionaries. No effort is made, however, to keep the service antique or in any way make it stagy. It is a popular devotional pageant, living, not 'revived,' and it has all the incongruities and irregularities that go with life as distinct from art.

Salads

Christmas Eve Salad

3 ORANGES, peeled and
    sectioned
3 BANANAS, peeled and sliced
1 GRAPEFRUIT, peeled
    and sectioned

1/2 cup PINE NUTS
1/2 cup GRENADINE
1 1/2 cups COCONUT, shredded

Mix all the ingredients together and refrigerate until ready to serve.

Serves 4 - 6.

Cranberry Salad

Linnie Taylor of Organ, New Mexico, gave us this recipe. Her mother, Ruth Harris, who has lived in Albuquerque over 60 years, makes this delicious salad every Christmas for family gatherings.

1 pkg. (16 oz.) CRANBERRIES
2 ORANGES, peeled and
    sectioned
2 RED APPLES, cored and
    chopped (leave peel on)
1 GREEN APPLE, cored and
    chopped (leave peel on)
1 1/2 cups SUGAR
RIND OF ONE ORANGE, grated

1 box RED RASPBERRY
    JELLO®
1 box BLACK RASPBERRY
    JELLO®
1 cup PECANS, chopped
1 cup crushed PINEAPPLE
LETTUCE
SOUR CREAM

Grind cranberries, oranges, and apples in a food processor or hand grinder. Stir sugar in and let stand for 1/2 hour. Add orange rind.

Make Jello using 3 1/2 cups water instead of the usual 4 cups. When Jello begins to set, add cranberry mixture, pineapple, and pecans. Chill in refrigerator until it sets up. Cut in 2 x 2 inch squares and serve on a bed of lettuce with a dollop of sour cream in which you have stirred some prepared cranberry relish.

Serves 8 - 10.

La Mesa Salad

I first enjoyed this unusual salad at a party in La Mesa. I've changed the recipe since, but I still remember it as "La Mesa Salad."

1 can (15 1/2 oz.) HOMINY, drained
2 cups PINTO BEANS, cooked and drained
4 or 5 GREEN ONIONS, chopped
1/4 cup PIMENTO, chopped
1 Tbsp. PARSLEY, chopped
3 Tbsp. SALAD OIL
1 Tbsp. BALSAMIC VINEGAR
1/4 cup prepared ITALIAN DRESSING
1 tsp. DIJON STYLE MUSTARD
1/2 tsp. ground RED CHILE POWDER
LETTUCE
1 cup CHEDDAR CHEESE, grated
SLICED BLACK OLIVES

Mix all ingredients together except lettuce, cheese, and olives. Line a large salad bowl with lettuce; fill with salad. Sprinkle cheese on top; garnish with black olives and serve.

Serves 6 - 8.

Lyndell Morris' Waldorf Salad

My mother-in-law, Lyndell Gean Morris, in her best southern tradition always prepared this salad for Christmas dinner.

2 cups APPLES, diced
1/2 LEMON
1 cup CELERY, diced
1 cup SEEDLESS GRAPES, cut in half
1 cup MAYONNAISE
1/2 cup SOUR CREAM
1/8 tsp. CARDAMON
1 cup PECANS, chopped

Squeeze lemon juice over apples. Add celery and grapes and mix lightly with mayonnaise, cardamon, and sour cream. Add pecans last, just before serving.

Serves 4 - 6.

Piñata Salad

1 can (20 oz.) PINEAPPLE
    CHUNKS
1 can (11 oz.) MANDARIN
    ORANGE SLICES
1/2 cup seedless GREEN
    GRAPES, cut in half
1/2 cup seedless RED GRAPES,
    cut in half

1/4 cup WHITE CRÈME DE
    MENTHE
1 cup flaked COCONUT
1 cup SOUR CREAM
LETTUCE LEAVES

Drain pineapple and mandarin oranges. Place in a large bowl. Add grapes and crème de menthe. Toss and chill for an hour. Fold in coconut and sour cream. Spoon onto a bed of lettuce and serve at once.

Serves 6 - 8.

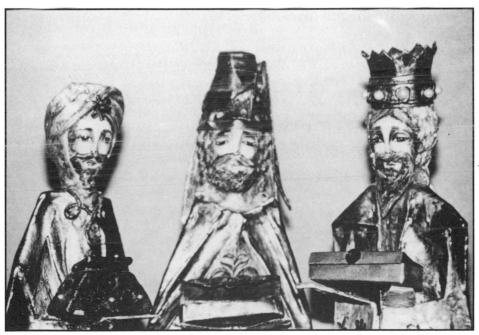

Three Wise Men

On the Twelfth Day of Christmas My True Love Gave to Me:

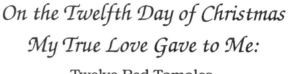

Twelve Red Tamales
Eleven Chile Rellenos
Ten Terrific Tacos
Nine Nifty Nachos
Eight Green Enchiladas
Seven Sopapillas
Six Fresh Tortillas
Five Margaritas
Four Empanadas
Three Jalapenos
Two Bean Burritos
And a Piñata in a Piñon Tree!

Chapter Three

Luminarias and Farolitos

Nothing separates Christmas in New Mexico more from those in the rest of the world than the lighting of farolitos and luminarias.

Although the custom has now spread to other parts of the country, people still come to New Mexico from all over the world to see the "little fires".

LUMINARIAS

In their hearts, New Mexicans believe

That the little fires they light on Christmas Eve

Will help Mary and Joseph find their way in the night

And bless those kind souls who set out the guiding light.

Old-timers and purists still argue about the difference between luminarias and farolitos. The matter has even been discussed in the New Mexico State Legislature.

As early as the sixteenth century, Indians in New Mexico were lighting bonfires made of twigs and branches, often from the native piñon tree, at Christmas time. These little fires, called luminarias, placed in front of the churches and pueblos were lit both in honor of the birth of Christ and to light the way for people to gather.

During the early 1800s, when the wagon trains traversed the Santa Fe trail from St. Louis to Santa Fe, new settlers brought small Chinese paper lanterns with them. They placed these around the fronts of their houses and hung them from the portals. Northern New Mexicans called these lights "farolitos" from the Spanish root word farol, meaning lantern or street lamp.

Because these lanterns were expensive and hard to come by, some creative souls began to devise different ways to accomplish the same purpose. One spin-off that survived, and is now used most often, is a small paper sack, often wax-lined, containing a small amount of sand or dirt and a votive candle embedded in the sand. The evolution continues still with the increasing use of plastic containers made to look like the traditional paper sack.

Currently there are even businesses in New Mexico that keep the plastic version on the roof line of their adobe buildings all year long.

Language, as we all know, changes over the years. Eventually, all except the most stalwart holdouts began calling the paper (or plastic) sacks with the votive candles in them—luminarias.

The term is particularly common in southern New Mexico, where we live. Therefore, taking everything into account, I have chosen to refer to these as luminarias in this book.

Little Fires on Christmas Eve - 1936

The Santa Fe New Mexican

Santa Fe, N.M.   Monday, December 17, 1909

On Christmas eve, the town was ablaze with bonfires, a beautiful custom centuries old and transplanted to New Mexico from Spain. The custom is observed each year and has been in vogue in this city fully three centuries.

Las Cruces Sun News

Las Cruces, New Mexico   December 19, 1939

FIESTA FEATURES WOOD HAULERS

SANTA FE. Dec. 19. Ritual of "La Fiesta de las Luminarias" (The Little Fires) and of the procession of wood haulers bringing piñon and cedar fuel for the fires to the Christ child will be observed according to tradition, on Christmas Eve, it was announced today.

Wood haulers, led by torch bearers, will drive the wood-laden burros to the cathedral to receive the blessing of the church before the fires are lighted on the plaza.

Albondigas Soup

This is our version of albondigas. At the Feast of Guadalupe, they serve the meatballs on the side. We prefer albondigas as a soup.

1 lb. GROUND BEEF
1 tsp. GARLIC SALT
1 tsp. ground RED CHILE
    POWDER
1 tsp. CILANTRO
1 tsp. CELERY SALT
1 cup dry BREAD CRUMBS
1 YELLOW ONION, chopped

1 EGG
1/4 cup WHITE WINE
1 Tbsp. TOMATO PASTE
2 cans (10 1/2 oz. each)
    BEEF BROTH
2 soup cans WATER
2 BAY LEAVES,
    broken in half

Mix together ground beef, garlic salt, chile powder, cilantro, celery salt, bread crumbs, onion, egg, wine, and tomato paste. Form into small balls. Pour beef broth and water into a large pan. Add bay leaves and bring broth to a boil. Add meatballs, a few at a time, so that boiling continues. After all the meatballs are in the pot, reduce heat, cover, and simmer for 45 minutes. Remove bay leaves before serving.

Serves 4 - 6.

Black Bean Soup

2 cups BLACK BEANS
2 quarts WATER
1 Tbsp. BACON DRIPPINGS
2 Tbsp. OLIVE OIL
1 small ONION, chopped
1 CARROT, diced
2 stalks CELERY, diced

1 Tbsp. PARSLEY, chopped
1 tsp. SALT
1/2 tsp. ground BLACK
    PEPPER
1/2 tsp. CAYENNE PEPPER
1 EGG, hard-boiled, chopped
1 LEMON, thinly sliced

Soak beans, in water to cover, overnight. Drain and rinse. Put bacon drippings and oil in a saucepan and saute onion for 5 minutes or until limp. Add beans, water, carrots, celery, parsley, salt, pepper, and cayenne. Simmer, over low heat, or in a crockpot for 4 hours. Let cool. Blend in a blender until smooth and put back into a saucepan. Warm over low heat until hot. Serve with a little chopped egg sprinkled on top and lemon slices.

Serves 6 - 8.

Cheese Soup

1/2 cup BUTTER
1/2 cup ONION, chopped
1/2 cup CELERY, chopped
1/4 cup all-purpose FLOUR
4 cups CHICKEN STOCK
2 cups MILK

1 can (12 oz.) BEER
1 cup VELVEETA®, diced
1/2 tsp. ground BLACK
    PEPPER
1/2 tsp. GARLIC SALT
1 Tbsp. PARSLEY, chopped

Melt butter in a pot large enough to hold all ingredients. Saute onions and celery over low heat until soft. Add flour and stir until mixture bubbles. Gradually add chicken stock and milk and stir until smooth. Add beer, cheese, garlic salt, and pepper. Cook over low heat until cheese melts and blends into mixture. Add parsley. Cook for 5 minutes more and serve hot. Great served with tortilla chips!

Serves 6 - 8.

Cream of Avocado Soup

3 large ripe AVOCADOS, peeled,
    pitted, and diced
1 1/2 cups CREAM
3 cups CHICKEN STOCK or
    BROTH
3 cups VEGETABLE STOCK*

1 clove GARLIC, minced
1/2 tsp. SALT
1 tsp. ground WHITE PEPPER
1/2 tsp. CAYENNE PEPPER
SOUR CREAM
2 Tbsp. CHIVES, chopped

Put avocados and cream in a blender and puree. Put the stocks in a saucepan and bring to a boil over high heat. Reduce heat; add avocado mixture, garlic, salt, and pepper. Cook over low heat, stirring until blended and hot. Serve with a dollop of sour cream, sprinkled with chives.

Serves 6 - 8

You can make your own vegetable stock using celery tops and other vegetables or peelings of your choice. You can also buy powdered vegetable stock from stores catering to vegetarians.

Pumpkin/Chile Soup

Most people think that the only thing you can make with pumpkin is a pie. It really is a most versatile vegetable. Here is a savory soup using two of my favorite things—pumpkin and chile.

1 2 to 2 1/2 pound PUMPKIN	1/2 cup GREEN CHILE, chopped
2 Tbsp. OIL	1/2 cup HAM, chopped
1 large ONION, chopped	1 tsp. ground BLACK PEPPER
2 cloves GARLIC, minced	1 tsp. ROSEMARY
4 cups CHICKEN BROTH	SALT to taste

Peel pumpkin; remove seeds and dice. Put oil in a large pot and brown the onion and garlic. Add diced pumpkin, chicken broth, chile, ham, pepper, and rosemary. Cook, over low heat, for 2 hours or until the soup is smooth and thick. Add salt to taste and serve hot.

Serves 6 - 8.

Soup Kitchen Soup

Occasionally Guylyn helps cook at a local soup kitchen. Area grocers and growers donate all sorts of wonderful fruits and vegetables. Since each week brings a different assortment of food stuffs, the soup is always different. This recipe evolved from this experience.

1 lb. stewing BEEF	4 YELLOW SQUASH, sliced
1 lb. cubed lean PORK	2 cups WHOLE KERNEL
3 Tbsp. OLIVE OIL	CORN
2 qts. CHICKEN STOCK or	2 ONIONS, chopped
BROTH	6 lg. GREEN CHILES, peeled,
3 qts. WATER	seeded, and chopped
6 POTATOES, cubed	2 JALAPENOS, chopped
6 SWEET POTATOES, cubed	SALT AND PEPPER

Lightly brown beef and pork in a large soup pot with olive oil. Add water and bring to a boil. Reduce heat, cover, and simmer for one hour. Add the remaining ingredients, including chicken stock, and cook for 30 more minutes or until the meat and vegetables are tender. Great served with garlic toast!

Serves 10-12

Chapter Four

Los Pastores

Los Pastores are religious folk plays dating from medieval times. These centuries-old mystery dramas were brought from Spain to Mexico by the Franciscan monks, probably to explain the story of Christmas to the Indians.

The plays later found their way to Nuevo (New) Mexico and continued being performed throughout the territory until the early twentieth century. Now Los Pastores are staged in only a few places around the state. Still, time has not dimmed their charm, and their spiritual wonder remains.

The story is a simple one—originally designed so that humble people could understand its message. Traditionally, Los Pastores were not written but verbally handed down from one generation to another.

The play opens with the devil, in the form of Lucifer, grotesquely made up. He is furious at Isaiah's prophecy of the coming of a savior. Other actors dressed as "diablitos," or little devils, dance around in a parody of evil wrath.

Next, a group of shepherds, tending their flocks, see the brilliant winter star announcing the birth of Christ. So they may welcome the Savior, they embark on their journey to Bethlehem.

Under protest, they drag along the drunken shepherd, Bartolo. While the other shepherds offer gifts and sing the praise of the Christ child, Bartolo drinks and nods off. However, upon seeing the baby Jesus, Bartolo casts off his life of sin and debauchery and offers his life to the service of Christ.

Everyone rejoices and the players sing "Noche Buena, Noche Santa" *(Silent Night.)* The audience joins in as the play comes to an end.

Afterwards, members of the cast and audience gather for refreshments.

Los Pastores are still popular in northern New Mexico and in Mesilla, in the southern part of the state near the Mexican border. The uniquely costumed actors originally performed in churches.

But they were relegated to presenting their play outside, in front of a church, as the dramas became too ribald to be performed inside a house of worship. Most presentations are once again performed inside churches—such as San Albino in Mesilla.

The basic ingredients of Los Pastores are the annunciation by the Arch angel of the birth of the Messiah, a chorus singing the "Gloria," a re-creation of the shepherds' journey to the manger in Bethlehem, and the offering of gifts referred to as the "adoration scene."

The Fransican friars, when introducing Christianity to the Indians of New Mexico, were struck by how easily the native Americans took to pageantry. The Indians even adapted it to their own ceremonial rites.

Early descendants of Spaniards, such as De Vargas or Onate and their followers, were often left to celebrate important holidays on their own. The few padres and missionaries were scattered throughout the large land expanse of the territory and unable to visit every mission or church as often as they wanted.

Therefore, the local parishioners would gather together, at a private home in the smaller villages or at someone's ranch, and undertake the production of Los Pastores. Many roles were often handed down from father to son, and the competition for these parts was extremely keen.

After the performance, the hosts of the evening would serve refreshments, usually in a room made comfortable by a roaring blaze in the fireplace.

The clash between good and evil, the costuming, humor, singing, camaraderie, good food, and good cheer all go to make Los Pastores an unforgettable part of the New Mexican holiday season.

Las Cruces Sun News

Las Cruces, New Mexico   December 24, 1939

Play 400 Years Old is Revived in L.C. Mesilla

Los Pastores, one of the oldest plays written in the New World almost 400 years ago, and produced through the centuries in Spanish-speaking America at Christmas time will be presented in Mesilla and in Las Cruces tonight.

The play in Mesilla will be given in two performances at the school house at 8 to 10 p.m. and again from 10 to 12 midnight.

The play in Las Cruces will be given in the auditorium at Loretto academy at 8 p.m.

Written for Indians

This old play, which has withstood the changes of the years, remains as popular as when written and produced by the Franciscan fathers in their efforts to make Indians understand the story of the Nativity.

The revival of interest in old customs, folklore and ancient rituals in New Mexico in connection with the Coronado Cuatro centennial is evident all over the state this year.

Story of Shepherds

Los Pastores is the story of the shepherds who watched their flocks by night and saw the star appear. The whole scene is built around the tiny bed in the manger but in the play is depicted the struggle between the angel and the devil, typifying one man's struggle between good and evil.

Mrs. Antonia Gonzales is directing the play given by members of St. Genevieve's church at the Loretto academy.

From Play to Mass

At Mesilla the audience and the cast will go from the last performance to St. Albino's church for midnight mass.

Alta Heath's Christmas Bread

Mrs. Heath is one of the best bakers I've ever encountered. This is her version of a stollen. It also reminds us of the wonderful Italian bread, Panettone.

1 tsp. HONEY
1 cup WARM WATER
6 Tbsp. granulated YEAST
2 cups MILK, scalded and
    cooled
1 lb. BUTTER, melted
2 cups HONEY
6 lg. EGGS
1/4 cup BRANDY or RUM
1/4 cup ORANGE PEEL, grated

11 cups all-purpose FLOUR
    (more if needed)
1 lb. WALNUTS, chopped (or
    slivered blanched
    almonds)
1 lb. assorted CANDIED
    FRUITS (no peels)
1 lb. RAISINS
1/2 tsp. ground MACE
1/2 tsp. NUTMEG

Using a machine with dough hook, in a large container, dissolve yeast in warm water with a teaspoon of honey. In mixing bowl, combine cooled milk, melted butter, honey, eggs, brandy or rum, orange peel, and flour. Mix, using dough hook, until all ingredients are thoroughly mixed. Stop machine and let dough rise. Add nuts, candied fruits, and raisins along with nutmeg and mace. Mix remaining ingredients until sides of bowl are clean, adding more flour at this point if necessary. The dough should be shiny and the shape of a basketball.

Alta Heath's Christmas Bread

Dump dough onto table and let rise slightly. Divide dough into loaves; shape into a thick oval shape. Lap the ovals over so that you have the traditional stollen shape.

Bake in a 350° oven for one hour or more. If some of the stollen are small, about 10 ounces, they may be baked for as little as 20 minutes. When bread is a pale blond color and done, remove from oven. Brush on a combination of melted butter and Kahlua, brandy, or rum while bread is still warm. You may sprinkle with powdered sugar, or make a frosting with powdered sugar, butter and Kahlua. Decorate with extra candied fruit or nuts. The dough can also be shaped into a wreath.

Horno Bread

(Indian Bread)

An horno (pronounced "or-no") is a wonderful beehive-shaped outdoor oven with a hole in the side for the bread and a hole in the top to let the smoke out.

2 pkgs. dry YEAST	**4 Tbsp. LARD or MARGARINE**
1/2 cup LUKEWARM WATER	**8 to 9 cups all-purpose**
1 Tbsp. SUGAR	**FLOUR**
2 tsp. SALT	

Stir yeast into lukewarm water. Add sugar and let stand for a few minutes until it softens. Mix salt into lard and add in yeast mixture and blend together. Add 1 cup of flour at a time, alternating with some of the water and blending thoroughly each time. Reserve some of the flour for kneading. When dough feels right, turn out on a board and knead until very smooth. Add more flour if dough gets sticky.

Cover and let stand in lightly greased bowl until double in bulk. Punch down and divide into four balls. Brush each with melted lard or margarine. Place in pie tins, cover, and let rise for about 30 minutes. Bake in a 350° oven for 50 minutes, until brown or when you thump bread, it sounds hollow.

Yield: 4 loaves.

Indian Fry Bread

2 cups all-purpose FLOUR
3 tsp. BAKING POWDER
1/2 tsp. SALT

WARM WATER,
      approx 3/4 cup
SHORTENING for frying

Mix together flour, baking powder, and salt. Add warm water to mixture and work into a smooth dough. Divide dough into balls about the size of a large egg. Roll each ball out on a lightly floured board until about 1/4-inch thick. Cut a small hole in the center of each circle.

Fry circles, one at a time, in 2 to 3 inches of shortening in a deep cast iron skillet. Turning once, fry circles until golden brown on both sides. Drain on paper towels.

Yield: 6 - 8 loaves.

Pumpkin Bread

1 cup BUTTER or MARGARINE
2 cups SUGAR
1 can (1 lb.) PUMPKIN
1/4 cup MOLASSES
3 cups all-purpose FLOUR
1 tsp. BAKING SODA
1 tsp. BAKING POWDER

1/2 tsp. SALT
3 tsp. ground CINNAMON
1 tsp. ground MACE
1 tsp. ground ALLSPICE
1 cup RAISINS
1 cup PECANS, chopped

Cream sugar and butter together. Add pumpkin and molasses and beat. Add flour, baking soda, baking powder, salt, cinnamon, mace, and allspice and beat again. Stir in raisins and pecans. Pour batter into a lightly greased and floured tube pan and bake in a 350 ° oven for 1 hour or until bread tests done with a toothpick.

Serves 8 - 10.

Three Kings Bread

(Rosca de Los Reyes)

Traditionally this bread, often called Rosca de Los Reyes (Three Kings Bread) is baked to celebrate Twelfth Night. Baked in a ring, the bread is garnished with "jewels" of nuts and candied fruit, symbolizing the jewels of the three kings.

Historically a tiny clay doll was hidden inside the bread before it was baked. More modern cooks often will make a small opening and wedge a little doll or some ornament in the bread after baking it.

The person who finds the treasure gets rewarded. The reward can be anything from getting the drumstick of the holiday bird, two pieces of Grandma's best pie, or being selected the one to play Santa Claus when the gifts are passed out.

THE DOUGH:

1 pkg. YEAST	1/4 cup SUGAR
1 tsp. SUGAR	1 tsp. SALT
1 cup warm MILK	1/4 cup MARGARINE, softened
3 to 3 1/2 cups WHITE BREAD FLOUR	2 EGGS

Dissolve yeast and 1 teaspoon of sugar in warm milk. Set aside for 5 to 10 minutes until foamy on top.

Add 3 cups of flour, 1/4 cup of sugar, salt, margarine, and eggs. Mix together until dough leaves the sides of bowl. Add more flour if necessary and knead about 5 minutes. Place dough in a lightly buttered bowl. Cover and let rise in warm place about 1 hour.

Turn dough out onto lightly floured board. Punch down and roll out with your hands into a 14 to 18 inch-long strip. Curl bread around and tuck ends under to make a circle. Place on lightly greased cookie sheet. Cover with buttered plastic wrap and let rise 1 hour. Remove wrap and bake in a 375° oven for about 30 minutes or until lightly browned.

Yield: 1 loaf.

See <u>ICING</u> and <u>GARNISH</u> next page . . .

THE ICING

1 1/2 cups POWDERED SUGAR　　**1 tsp. VANILLA**
3 Tbsp. MILK　　　　　　　　　　**HOT WATER**
1 Tbsp. SHERRY WINE

Combine all ingredients except water. Beat until smooth. Add enough hot water to make a spreadable icing.

GARNISH:

1/2 cup CANDIED FRUIT　　**1 tiny DOLL or JELLY BEAN**
1/4 cup PECANS, chopped　　　**ORNAMENT**
1/4 cup RAISINS

When bread is cool, cut slit in side to insert the tiny doll. Drizzle icing over and around bread, making sure to cover the slit. Decorate with candied fruit, raisins, and nuts.

Three
Kings
Bread

Chapter Five

La Noche Buena
(Christmas Eve)

New Mexicans celebrate Christmas Eve in a myriad of ways. The entire family piles into the car and spends several hours looking at the luminarias; friends and neighbors embark on a posada; and people attend church services including midnight mass. Many people in the state entertain on Christmas Eve. We've been to everything from open houses and cocktail parties to formal sit-down dinners and a winter barbecue.

The Spanish-speaking people of New Mexico call Christmas Eve "La Noche Buena," which literally means "the good night." I've always thought that it was a wonderful way to express the attitude most New Mexicans have towards the day before Christmas.

One can feel it start at about noon. Retail stores are, of course, extremely busy. But most other businesses start gearing up to gear down. There are a lot of people out and about—delivering gifts of all sorts to their friends and business acquaintances: poinsettias, boxes of homemade candies and cookies, bottles of liquor, hand-knit scarves, or some small memento bought at a gift shop.

One can also hear people saying over and over to themselves or anyone who will listen, "I've got to go to mass tonight . . . I've got to get everything done so I can go to mass tonight."

I have heard midnight mass referred to by old-timers as "la Misa del Gallo," which roughly translated means "the Mass of the Rooster." I was intrigued by this seemingly irreverent name for such a solemn ceremony.

Folklore has it that, on the night Jesus was born, the animals around the manger were dismayed because there were no human visitors to the site to observe this momentous happening. The donkey and the ox did their part to celebrate the occasion by supplying warmth to the infant with their breath.

Outside, an aging rooster flew to a high point near the manger and, in his own way, announced the birth of the Christ child. It then seems another rooster joined in. Thus, Spanish-speaking peoples, passing this tale down through the ages, began to call the mass "la Misa del Gallo" in honor of the first announcers of the coming of the Messiah.

We met a marvelous old lady on one of our sojourns in San Jose. We fondly recall several of the stories she told us about "the good old days" in New Mexico.

She said that, until the Thirties, it was customary for groups of young boys to gather every Christmas Eve and go from house to house "asking Oremus."

The young men sang little verses all beginning with "Oremus," a Latin word used to introduce a liturgical prayer in the Roman Catholic church.

Some of those boys were holy terrors all year, breaking windows and stealing fruit from other people's trees. But when Christmas Eve came around they would act like little angels. They would stand outside their neighbors' houses singing Christmas carols in high, shrill tones—because their voices had yet to change. Then the lady of the house would give them cookies and other special goodies she had baked especially for them.

Nuestra Senora Refugio
de Pecadores
(Our Lady of Refuge)

Main Dishes

Baked Fresh Ham with Apple Cider

This is wonderful for a holiday buffet. Slice thinly and serve with a gravy made from the drippings.

Preheat oven to 325°.

1 FRESH HAM, 10 - 14 lbs.
1 tsp. SAGE
1 tsp. ground BLACK PEPPER
1 Tbsp. MARJORAM
2 cups APPLE CIDER

3 Tbsp. BUTTER
3 Tbsp. FLOUR
2 Tbsp. APPLE BRANDY
2 cups CHICKEN BROTH

Score ham with a knife, making a diamond pattern. Mix together sage, black pepper, and marjoram and rub into surface of ham. Place meat on a rack in a large roasting pan. Pour apple cider over meat and roast, uncovered, for 3 hours or until done. Baste about every 30 minutes. Skim fat from the pan drippings. Make a roux with butter and flour. Add pan drippings, apple brandy, and chicken broth to make the gravy. Serve gravy on the side.
Serves 12 - 16.

Baked Ham with Tequila

The butt portion of half HAM
    (approx. 5 1/2 to 7 lbs.)
2 dozen whole CLOVES
8 oz. ORANGE MARMALADE
2 Tbsp. PREPARED MUSTARD

1/2 tsp. ground CLOVES
1/2 tsp. ground NUTMEG
1/2 tsp. ground ALLSPICE
1 cup TEQUILA

Wash ham well in cold water (this helps remove any excess salt.) Stick cloves in ham and put into a large baking pan. In a saucepan, mix together the rest of the ingredients, except the tequila. Cook over very low heat, stirring constantly until blended together. Add half of the tequila. Cook until the sauce is smooth. Stir in the rest of the tequila and pour over the ham. Bake in a 325 ° oven for 2 to 2 1/2 hours, basting occasionally. Slice the ham and serve with the sauce on the side.

Serves 6 - 8.

Baked Sliced Ham with Sauces

When visitors come calling, a sliced Christmas ham and Mexican rolls or bolillos, and various condiments make a wonderful "cushion" for some of the libations they may consume during the evening.

1/2 bone-in HAM (8-10 pounds)
1 cup WATER
1/2 cup ORANGE-FLAVORED
    LIQUEUR

1/2 cup ORANGE JUICE
2 tsp. ground CLOVES

Put ham in a large baking pan. Mix water, liqueur, orange juice, and cloves together and pour over ham. Bake in a 325° oven for 2 hours, basting occasionally, until done. Let cool and slice. Arrange on a platter and surround with the following sauces.

Cumberland Sauce Variation

1 cup MAYONNAISE
2 Tbsp. PREPARED MUSTARD
1 Tbsp. CURRANT JELLY
Mix well with a wire whisk until smooth.

Makes approx. 1 cup.

Christmas Mustard

1 cup CHAMPAGNE or DRY WHITE WINE
1 Tbsp. DRY MUSTARD
3 EGGS
Pinch CAYENNE PEPPER
Combine wine and mustard. Beat eggs and cayenne together. Combine mixtures in top of a double broiler over boiling water. Cook and stir until thickened. Remove from heat and refrigerate.

Makes approx. 1 1/2 cups.

Pecos Trail Sauce

1 Tbsp. HORSERADISH
1 cup SOUR CREAM
1 tsp. DILLWEED, chopped
Mix all ingredients together. Refrigerate for one hour before serving.

Makes approx. 1 cup.

Hacienda Sauce

1 cup PEACH JAM
1/4 cup seedless RAISINS, plumped*
2 Tbsp. BOURBON

Mix all ingredients together. Chill in refrigerator for one hour before serving.

*To plump the raisins - put them into a saucepan with water to cover. Bring to a boil; remove from heat and let stand 10 minutes. Drain before using.

Makes approx. 1 1/4 cups.

Boneless Chicken Breast

with

Tequila Chile Sauce

When I first started writing my now-syndicated food column many years ago, this was the first recipe I used. I've adapted it since but, perhaps, I was on the right track in the beginning, since I'm still using it!

1 lb. CHICKEN BREASTS,
    boneless, skinned
1/2 cup all-purpose FLOUR
1 Tbsp. PAPRIKA
1 tsp. ground WHITE PEPPER
1/4 cup BUTTER

2 Tbsp. OLIVE OIL
3 GREEN ONIONS, chopped
1/2 cup GREEN CHILE,
    chopped
1/2 cup TEQUILA
1/2 cup CREAM

Pound chicken breasts until approximately 3/4-inch thick. Mix flour, paprika, and pepper together and dredge chicken in flour. Melt butter in a frying pan. Add oil and saute green onions for 2 minutes. Add chicken breasts and chile. Cook, over medium heat, 10 to 12 minutes or until done. Remove chicken to a warm platter.

Deglaze pan with tequila and cook, over medium high heat, until liquid is reduced by half. Add cream. Reduce heat and cook until warm and slightly thickened. Pour over chicken breasts and serve.

Serves 4 - 6.

Canyon Road Eggs Benedict

Sunday brunch is a given in Santa Fe. Whether in one of the many fine restaurants or at home—it is just one more of the city's enjoyable customs. This is my version of the classic Eggs Benedict—perfect not only for a Sunday brunch, but also great for Christmas morning breakfast.

4 ENGLISH MUFFINS
8 slices CANADIAN BACON
8 EGGS

GUACAMOLE HOLLANDAISE
BLACK OLIVE SLICES
CHOPPED PIMENTO

Toast the English muffins and place the two halves on each plate. Lightly saute Canadian bacon and top each muffin half with a slice. Poach eggs and top each slice of bacon with one egg. Pour Guacamole Hollandaise sauce over them. Garnish with black olive slices and pimento and serve.

Guacamole Hollandaise

2 ripe AVOCADOS
1 cup MAYONNAISE

2 Tbsp. LIME JUICE
Tabasco® to taste

Mash avocados; whip in mayonnaise, lime juice, and Tabasco with a wire whisk until smooth. Pour over Eggs Benedict.

Serves 4.

Carne Adobada

Carne Adobada is pork chops marinated in red chile sauce. If you like hot, hot food try this!

12 RED CHILE PODS, dried
1-1/2 cups WATER
1 clove GARLIC, minced
1 tsp. OREGANO

1/2 tsp. CUMIN
1 tsp. SALT
6 PORK CHOPS
2 Tbsp. COOKING OIL

Crush red chile pods in a blender. Add water, and blend until smooth. Run mixture through a strainer to take out seeds and skin. Cook in a saucepan with the seasonings until mixture comes to a boil. Pour over pork chops. Cover and refrigerate overnight. Remove chops and reserve marinade. Brown chops in oil on both sides. Pour marinade over them and cook, covered, over low heat 30 to 45 minutes or until done.

Serves 4 - 6.

Celebration Pork Chops

1 Tbsp. COOKING OIL
4 large PORK CHOPS
1 cup RICE
1/2 cup VERMICELLI, broken
        into pieces
1/2 cup TOMATO, chopped
1/4 cup ONION, chopped

1/4 cup GREEN CHILE,
        chopped
3 cups WATER
1/2 tsp. GARLIC SALT
1/2 tsp. ground RED CHILE
        POWDER

Brown pork chops on both sides in oil. Remove from frying pan and reserve. Brown rice and vermicelli in pork drippings. Put pork chops back in pan, add tomato, onion, chile, water, garlic salt, and red chile powder. Bring to a boil over high heat. Lower heat to simmer and cook, covered, for 45 minutes or until pork chops are done.

Serves 4.

Christmas Tamales

This is a simplified version of green chile, cheese tamales.

18 dried CORN HUSKS
1 cup MASA HARINA*
1/2 tsp. BAKING POWDER
1 cup SHOE PEG CORN, cooked
and drained
1/3 cup VEGETABLE OIL
1 cup MONTEREY JACK
CHEESE, shredded

1/2 cup GREEN CHILE,
chopped
1/4 cup PIMENTOS, chopped
1/2 tsp. SALT
1 tsp. CUMIN
1 Tbsp. CILANTRO, finely
chopped

Soak dried corn husks in warm water for an hour before using; drain and trim square. Mix rest of ingredients together and blend well. The dough will be sticky. Divide dough equally and place into the center of each corn husk. Fold the two sides of the husk into the middle, then fold in the top and bottom.

Stand tamales, on end, on a rack in steamer, over approximately an inch of hot water. Cover and steam over medium heat for 1 hour, adding more water if necessary.

Yield: 18 tamales.

*Can be purchased in supermarkets in the Southwest, Mexican stores or specialty gourmet shops in other parts of the country.

Christmas Turkey
with
White Wine Basting Sauce

Years ago, many cooks would put a turkey in the oven on very low and cook it all night and wonder why it dried out. I use the following method of cooking a turkey—which I adapted from the technique used by my good friend June Traeger, a syndicated food columnist and one of the best cooks I've ever met.

Preheat oven to 500°.

**1 TURKEY (I usually use a
    20-lb bird)**
1 cup dry WHITE WINE
1/2 tsp. NUTMEG, ground
1/2 tsp. CLOVES, ground

**1/2 tsp. WHITE PEPPER,
    ground**
2 Tbsp. BUTTER, melted
1 cup CHICKEN BROTH
1 cup WATER

Wash the turkey thoroughly and put on a rack or slotted tray inside a large roasting pan. Mix together the rest of the ingredients and pour over turkey. Cover the turkey with heavy-duty aluminum foil and bake in a preheated 500° oven as follows:

    First half-hour — 500°
    Second half-hour — 450°
    Third half-hour — 400°

Turn down heat to 350° and continue cooking turkey for one more hour. Remove foil. (You may want to wrap the legs with foil if they are getting too brown.) Baste turkey with pan drippings 2 or 3 times as it continues to cook. It will take about 1 1/2 hours more cooking time at 350° to finish the bird (remember this is a 20-pound bird.) To test if the bird is done—move the legs up and down. If they move very easily, it is done.

Remove from oven. Take turkey out of pan and let sit for 1/2 to 1 hour loosely covered with foil. It will be easier to slice when cooled slightly.

Let pan drippings cool for about 1/2 hour. Skim off fat and any unsightly pieces. Make a roux with equal parts flour and butter and use the drippings along with some milk to make your gravy.

Ham Mousse

2 cups diced, cooked HAM
2 EGG YOLKS
1/4 tsp. ground NUTMEG
1/2 tsp. DIJON STYLE
     MUSTARD

1/4 tsp. RED CHILE POWDER
1 cup CREAM
2 Tbsp. DRY SHERRY
2 EGG WHITES

Run diced ham through finest blade of a food processor or chopper. Beat egg yolks; then add to the ham along with nutmeg, mustard, and chile powder. Beat cream until just stiff; then stir in sherry. Fold into ham mixture. Beat egg whites until stiff and fold into the mixture. Put into a lightly buttered souffle dish and bake in a 325° oven for one hour or until firm. Serve at once with Hollandaise Sauce.

Serves 4.

Hollandaise Sauce

1/4 lb. BUTTER, divided in half
2 EGG YOLKS, lightly beaten

1 Tbsp. LEMON JUICE
dash of CAYENNE PEPPER

Place half of the butter in a small saucepan with egg yolks and lemon juice in the top of a double boiler over hot (not boiling) water. Stir mixture constantly until butter melts. Add rest of the butter and continue stirring until mixture thickens. Remove from top of double boiler and stir in cayenne pepper. Serve at once.

Yield: approx. one-half cup.

Holiday Chicken Livers

We've known Marc Sebastian, a very talented entertainer, longer than any of us care to admit. He spends Christmas with us, in New Mexico, as often as his busy schedule permits. He's mad for chicken livers, and this is one of the ways we make them for him.

1 lb. CHICKEN LIVERS
3 Tbsp. BUTTER
1 tsp. PAPRIKA
1 Tbsp. all-purpose FLOUR
1/2 cup BEEF BROTH
1/4 cup CREAM

2 Tbsp. PORT WINE
1/2 tsp. ground WHITE
    PEPPER
1/2 tsp. SALT
1 tsp. PARSLEY, chopped

Wash, cut in half, and dry chicken livers. Melt butter in a large frying pan; sprinkle chicken livers with paprika, and saute for 8 to 10 minutes over medium heat or until done to taste. Remove to a warm platter and keep warm. Stir flour into pan, adding more butter if necessary to make a roux. Then slowly stir in beef broth. Add port, cream, parsley, salt and pepper. Heat through. Pour over chicken livers and serve. Good spooned over rice or toast points.

Serves 4.

Pork Scallopine Cilantro

Many chefs, seeking to escape the hustle and bustle and the confines of other sections of the country, come to Santa Fe. And using the centuries-old cuisine of the area, they try to improve upon it. Some of these recipes add an interesting twist to what is already a fascinating manner of cooking. The following is one such recipe.

8 pieces of PORK SCALOPPINE, pounded
1 Tbsp. BUTTER
1 Tbsp. OLIVE OIL
1/2 Tbsp. PARSLEY, chopped

1 CLOVE GARLIC, minced
1/4 tsp. WHITE PEPPER, ground
1/2 Tbsp. PAPRIKA

Melt butter in large frying pan, then add oil. Stir spices into pan. Add pork scaloppines and saute for 1 to 2 minutes on each side or until just done. Do not overcook or they will become tough. Serve with Cilantro Hollandaise (make a traditional hollandaise sauce, add 1 teaspoon chopped cilantro).

Serves 4.

Posole de Posada

There are many New Mexicans who do not feel Christmas Eve or New Year's Day is complete without several bowls of posole complemented with a fiery red chile sauce. A "Dona" of San Juan insisted that posole was most appropriate at Christmas time. When she learned of our great love of cooking, she verbally gave me this recipe, which was hastily scribbled on a napkin. It is one of the best versions of posole we've ever tasted.

**2 Tbsp. BACON DRIPPINGS
    or COOKING OIL
1 large ONION, chopped
3 cloves GARLIC, minced
1 1/2 lb. lean PORK, cubed
1 1/2 tsp. dried OREGANO
2 tsp. CUMIN**

**2 BAY LEAVES
1/2 cup WHITE WINE
1/2 cup WATER
1 can (#10) WHITE HOMINY
    with the juice
1 cup GREEN CHILE,
    chopped**

Heat the bacon drippings or oil in a heavy frying pan. Saute onion, garlic, and cubed pork, stirring occasionally, until pork is browned. Add oregano, cumin, and bay leaves. Pour the wine and water into the pan. Cover and cook for 30 minutes.

Put the hominy (with the liquid) in a large pot. Add green chile and the pork mixture (with liquid). Cook, over low heat for at least one hour. Remove bay leaves and serve in soup bowls with the following Red Chile Sauce on the side.

Serves 10 - 12.

Guylyn's Very Own
Red Chile Sauce

Guylyn, who has lived in New Mexico, for most of her life, has experimented with many red chile sauces. This particular one is her favorite. Although many New Mexican purists may throw up their arms in horror at some of the additions, it is by far the best I've ever tasted.

24 dried RED CHILE PODS*
4 to 5 cups WATER
2 tsp. CUMIN
2 tsp. SALT

2 cloves GARLIC, minced
1/4 cup DRIED ONION FLAKES
1 can (8 oz.) TOMATO SAUCE

Blend chile pods, a few at a time, in a blender with 1 cup water. Then strain through a sieve. Put the juice in a saucepan then repeat the process. When finished, add the rest of the ingredients and cook over low heat for 15 minutes. Store in the refrigerator or pour into small containers and freeze.

* We use medium hot chile. But you may use mild to very hot, depending on your taste.

Red Chile Chicken

Preheat oven to 350°

4 CHICKEN BREASTS, with
   skin removed
1 cup ITALIAN SEASONED
   BREAD CRUMBS
2 tsp. RED CHILE powder

1 tsp. GARLIC POWDER
1 tsp. ground BLACK
   PEPPER
1 tsp. grated LEMON RIND
2 Tbsp. OLIVE OIL

Rinse chicken under cold water and pat dry. Put bread crumbs, chile powder, garlic powder, pepper, and lemon rind in a plastic bag and mix well. Coat chicken with olive oil. Shake 1 piece at a time in the mixture. Lightly spray a black iron skillet or a baking dish with natural vegetable coating. Place chicken in it and bake, uncovered, for 45 minutes or until tender.

Serves 4.

Red Chile Tamales

CHILE CON CARNE (Red Chile Meat):

**2 lbs. PORK LOIN, cut in
    small cubes**
2 Tbsp. all-purpose FLOUR
2 Tbsp. COOKING OIL
**2 cups RED CHILE SAUCE
    (or 6 Tbsp. CHILE POWDER
    and 2 cups beef broth)**

1 ONION, chopped
1 tsp. SALT
1 tsp. OREGANO
1 tsp. CUMIN
1 clove GARLIC, minced
1 cup crushed TOMATOES

Trim fat from the meat and shake in a bag with flour. Brown meat and onions in oil. Add all other ingredients. Cook over very low heat for 1 hour or until the meat is tender. (If you use chile powder add 2 cups of beef broth.) This mixture must be thick to go in the tamales.

DOUGH:

1 cup LARD
1 tsp. SALT
5 cups MASA HARINA*
1 Tbsp. BAKING SODA

**3 cups WARM WATER
    (may need more to
    make dough pliable)**

Whip the lard and salt until light and fluffy. Add masa harina, baking soda and warm water; mix together well. Add more water if necessary to make dough sticky, so it will adhere to corn husks .

ASSEMBLING THE TAMALES:

2 to 3 dozen CORN HUSKS

Soak corn husks in warm water until they are soft and pliable. Trim edges square.

Spread corn husks with cornmeal mixture about 1/2-inch thick. Put 1 or 2 tablespoons chile con carne in center. Fold the 2 sides together, then the top and bottom. Stand the tamales, on end and close enough together so that tamales do not come unwrapped, on a rack in steamer over 1 inch of hot water. Cover and steam over medium heat for 1 hour. Add water periodically.

*Can be purchased in supermarkets in the Southwest, Mexican stores or specialty gourmet shops in other parts of the country.

Roast Chicken
with
Sage Stuffing

2 to 2 1/2 lb. ROASTING CHICKEN
1 Tbsp. SALT

Soak chicken in water to cover with salt for 1/2 hour. Rinse with cold water and stuff with the following Sage Stuffing. Bake in a 400 ° oven for 15 minutes. Reduce heat to 325° and cook 45 minutes to 1 hour or until done. Baste twice with the butter mixed with paprika.

Sage Stuffing

3 Tbsp. BUTTER or MARGARINE
1/2 ONION, chopped
2 stalks CELERY, chopped
1 Tbsp. PARSLEY, chopped
2 cups BREAD CRUMBS
1 tsp. SALT

1/4 tsp. CAYENNE PEPPER
2 tsp. SAGE
1/2 tsp. NUTMEG
1/4 cup CHICKEN BROTH
1 Tbsp. TEQUILA or
WHITE WINE

Melt butter in a frying pan and saute onion and celery until limp. Mix with rest of the ingredients. Stuff chicken and roast as per above instructions. (Or, if you prefer, bake the stuffing separately in a lightly greased oven-proof casserole dish.) When baking the chicken without the stuffing, you may have to reduce cooking time for the chicken.

Serves 4 - 6.

Roast Goose

My father's family clung to their English origins and this showed up in some of my father's habits. He eschewed ice in his drinks, was an avid sportsman, liked port wine, and did not think Christmas was complete without roast goose for dinner.

Preheat oven to 325°

**1 GOOSE, approximately
    12 pounds
1/4 cup BUTTER melted
1 can (1 lb., 13 oz.) SPICED
    PEACHES**

**1/2 cup PORT WINE
1 cup WATER**

Wash goose and trim off any excess fat. Prick the skin with tines of a sharp fork, then rub melted butter into the skin. Stuff cavity with peaches, reserving the juice. Place the goose, breast side up, on a rack inside a large roasting pan. Mix together port with the reserved peach juice and water and put in bottom of the roasting pan.

Bake goose in a 325° oven for 2 1/2 hours or until meat thermometer, inserted deep inside breast, reads 180°.

Remove goose from pan, discard peaches, and cover with aluminum foil. Let set for 30 minutes before carving.

GRAVY:

**1/2 cup PORT WINE
1 Tbsp. CORNSTARCH
1 to 2 cups CHICKEN STOCK**

Skim fat from drippings. Dissolve cornstarch in the wine and stir into drippings. Cook over low heat, adding chicken stock until gravy thickens. Serve with sliced Roast Goose.

Roast Pork
with
Cranberry-Chile Sauce

There are not many cuts of meat I'd rather have than a wonderful pork roast. I often cook it with fruit, and the combination of cranberry and chile makes a perfect holiday main course.

3 1/2 to 4 lb. boneless PORK ROAST
1 tsp. ROSEMARY
1 can (1 lb.) whole berry CRANBERRY SAUCE
1/4 cup LIME JUICE

1/2 tsp. CAYENNE PEPPER
1/4 cup GREEN CHILE, chopped
2 cloves GARLIC, minced
1 tsp. ground BLACK PEPPER

Place the roast in a baking pan; rub rosemary into it and bake in a 400° oven for 1 hour. Mix the rest of the ingredients together and pour over the roast. Reduce oven heat to 325°. Bake for 1 1/2 more hours or until done, basting with the cranberry mixture at least 3 times.

Serves 6 - 8.

Roast Turkey Breast
with
Pomegranate Sauce

A lot of people would prefer to cook a turkey breast rather than a whole turkey. They either don't like the dark meat of the turkey or they don't have a large family or group to feed.

Pomegranates grow in New Mexico and make a wonderful sauce to serve with the turkey breast.

> **1 whole TURKEY BREAST 4 to 5 lb**
> **1 cup WATER**
> **2 Tbsp. WHITE WINE**
> **VEGETABLE OIL**

Place the turkey breast in a pan that has a rack or a drip pan. Put approximately 1 cup of water and 2 tablespoons of white wine in bottom of pan. Rub vegetable oil over turkey breast, cover with aluminum foil and cook for 30 minutes in a 450° oven. Reduce the heat to 400°; cook for 30 more minutes. Reduce the heat to 350°. Remove the aluminum foil and cook for 1 to 1/2 hours more or until the turkey breast is done.

Serves 6 - 8.

Pomegranate Sauce

2 Tbsp. WATER
2 tsp. CORNSTARCH
1 cup CHICKEN BROTH
1 clove GARLIC, run through
    a garlic press

Juice from 4 or 5 POMEGRAN-
    ATES or 1 can pome-
    granate juice
1/2 tsp. NUTMEG
1/2 tsp. CUMIN

Stir cornstarch into water until dissolved. Place the rest of the ingredients in a saucepan. Stir in cornstarch and cook, over low heat, until thickened. Serve with sliced Roast Turkey Breast.

Stuffed Loin of Pork

2 Tbsp. BUTTER	1/2 lb. CHORIZO SAUSAGE*
1/2 ONION, chopped	1/2 cup PIÑON NUTS (Pine Nuts)
2 cloves GARLIC, minced	1 cup BREAD CRUMBS
1 tsp. ground BLACK PEPPER	3 - 3 1/2 lb. PORK LOIN ROAST
1 Tbsp. PARSLEY, chopped	

Melt butter in a frying pan, add onion, garlic, pepper, and parsley. Remove chorizo from its casing and crumble into pan. Saute until chorizo is lightly browned and onion is soft. Remove from heat; stir in piñons and bread crumbs. Lay pork roast out flat and spoon bread and chorizo mixture onto one side of the roast. Fold the other half over and tie with butcher's string. Put into a roasting pan and bake for 2 hours in a 350° oven or until the roast is done.

Serves 4 - 6.

*Chorizo is a very spicy, hot sausage seasoned with red chile. If not available in your area, substitute regular sausage or hot Italian sausage and add red chile powder, to taste, to the sausage.

Turkey Enchiladas

2 Tbsp. OLIVE OIL
1 YELLOW ONION, chopped
2 cups white TURKEY MEAT,
    cooked and chopped
1 can (10 3/4 oz.) CREAM of
    MUSHROOM SOUP
1 can (10 3/4 oz.) CREAM of
    CELERY SOUP
1 soup can MILK

1 cup GREEN CHILE,
    chopped
2 cloves GARLIC, minced
1/2 tsp. CUMIN
COOKING OIL
1 doz. CORN TORTILLAS
1/2 lb. LONGHORN CHEESE,
    grated

Heat a saucepan; add olive oil, then saute onions until soft. Stir in turkey, soup, milk, chile, garlic, and cumin. Cook, over low heat, until warm. Heat just enough cooking oil in a skillet to lightly coat each tortilla. Turn tortillas in hot oil until just soft and set aside.

In a lightly greased baking dish (9 x 13 inch), layer tortillas four at a time, alternating with one-third each of the soup mixture and the cheese. Top off with cheese each time. Bake in a 350 ° oven for 30 minutes or until hot and bubbly.

Serves 4 - 6.

Upside-Down Ham Loaf

2 Tbsp. BUTTER

Melt butter in microwave and pour into a 2-quart microwave-safe baking ring.

1/2 cup crushed PINEAPPLE

Drain well and reserve the juice. Spread the pineapple over the butter.

2 EGGS, lightly beaten
2 Tbsp. ONION, chopped
2 Tbsp. GREEN BELL PEPPER, chopped
1 Tbsp. PARSLEY, chopped
2 tsp. PREPARED MUSTARD
1/4 tsp. ground CLOVES
1/2 cup unseasoned BREAD CRUMBS

1/2 cup PINEAPPLE JUICE (use the juice reserved from the pineapple)
4 cups cooked HAM, ground
several dashes TABASCO® (optional)
ENDIVE (for garnish)

Mix all of the ingredients. Pack into baking ring and cook in microwave for 15 minutes on full power or until done. Use a turntable or rotate the ring a quarter of a turn every 3 minutes. Let stand 5 minutes and turn out onto a serving plate or platter. Garnish with endive and serve.

Serves 8.

Chapter Six

Piñatas and Piñons

Many children in New Mexico believe Christmas is not complete without a piñata! The piñata is a tradition used at children's birthday parties. So what could be more appropriate than to have a piñata at the birthday of the Christ child?

The piñata festivities begin with the children gathered together in an open area. The filled piñata is suspended so that it will swing overhead. A child is blindfolded and given a stick. Then, to the delight of the other children assembled, the child tries to hit the piñata and break it open. After two or three futile attempts, another child gets a couple of swings. This continues until one lucky youngster whacks the piñata hard enough to break it open. All sorts of candies and gifts spill out and everyone shares in the treats.

In the past, piñatas were limited in motif to such figures as donkeys and stars. Today, however, one can buy fanciful designs including Mickey Mouse®, Superman®, Santa Claus, Elves, Angels, and even Ninja Turtles®.

Traditional piñatas were clay bowls that broke when hit. Now piñatas are constructed of papier-maché, covered with brightly colored, shredded tissue paper.

Although we read that the Italians claim to have had the first piñata—before the Spaniards brought the custom to Mexico—nothing is more Mexican and New Mexican than one of these gaily decorated figures stuffed with goodies.

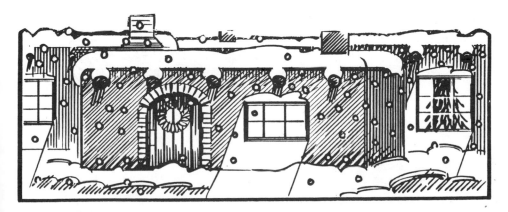

We found the following description of children enjoying the delights of a piñata.

Mesilla News

La Mesilla, New Mexico   September 1, 1938

While in no way officially connected with the novena, the custom is that the ceremony be followed with a Piñata for the children.

An olla is filled with candy and nuts and suspended over the center of the cement porch of the church, and a blindfolded child is given a baseball bat and makes an effort to break the jar. There is great excitement among the children awaiting the scramble for the contents of the olla and many are the directions shrieked at the blindfolded one. But with fifty excited kids yelling directions all at once, it is not easy to follow and it generally requires several attempts by different children before some lucky one connects with the swinging piñata, and a shower of goodies drop to the pavement. Then comes a demonstration of diving on the cement which would make Aileen Riggin envious, as the children swarm for the candy.

The piñon tree, a native evergreen, has long been the traditional choice for a New Mexico Christmas tree. Piñon nuts are prized additions to New Mexican cooking and used in a wide variety of dishes including candy, salads, and main dishes.

These tiny piñon or pine nuts have a distinct flavor unlike the nuts more commonly used in cooking. Although difficult to harvest, hard to shell, and expensive to buy in stores, they are well worth it.

Often lavish decorations adorn the Christmas trees in our New Mexico homes. One sees trees decked out in an array of ornamentation, from store-bought colored balls to milagros, hand-woven straw angels, and, of course, red and green chile peppers.

Handmade gifts and decorations are extremely prized and often passed down from one generation to another. A tree that stands out in our minds was completely decorated in angels made from lace and linen handkerchiefs. It had been crafted by a northern New Mexican family this way since the late 1800s.

PRAYERFUL ANGEL

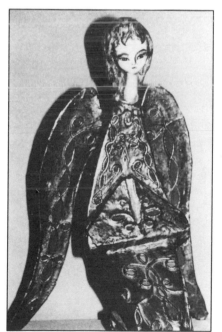

PAPIER-MÂCHÉ ANGEL

Blue Corn Meal Pancakes

Blue corn meal is used in the northern part of New Mexico more than in the southern part. Like olives, martinis, and rhubarb, it is an acquired taste—but one well worth going to the effort of getting to know.

1 cup BLUE CORNMEAL	1 1/2 cups MILK
1 cup all-purpose FLOUR	2 EGGS, well beaten
2 tsp. BAKING POWDER	1/2 cup vegetable OIL
1/2 tsp. SALT	

Mix together blue corn meal, flour, baking powder, and salt in a mixing bowl. Stir in milk, then the eggs and beat. Slowly beat in the oil. Drop by tablespoon onto a hot griddle.

SERVE WITH:

1/2 cup SOUR CREAM
1/4 cup GREEN CHILE, chopped

Mix sour cream and green chile together. Using a small ice cream scoop, put a scoopful on top of each stack of pancakes. This makes a great side dish for your "authentic" Christmas table.

Yield: approx. 12 pancakes.

Brandied Sweet Potatoes

4 medium-size SWEET POTATOES	2 Tbsp. BUTTER
	1/2 tsp. SALT
1/2 cup LIGHT BROWN SUGAR	1/2 tsp. WHITE PEPPER
1/4 cup ORANGE JUICE	1 Tbsp. BRANDY

Boil the sweet potatoes in lightly salted water until tender. Let cool slightly in order to handle and peel. Mix together brown sugar, orange juice, butter, salt, and pepper and cook over low heat for 10 minutes. Remove from heat and stir in brandy. Put sweet potatoes in a glass or ceramic baking dish. Pour the brandy mixture over them. Bake in a 325° oven for 30 minutes.
Serves 4.

Broccoli
with
Almond Butter Sauce

1/2 lb. FRESH BROCCOLI	**1/2 cup slivered ALMONDS**
OR	**1 Tbsp. LEMON JUICE**
1 10 oz. pkg. FROZEN BROCCOLI	**2 Tbsp. sliced RIPE OLIVES**
SPEARS	**1 Tbsp. chopped PIMENTO**
4 Tbsp. BUTTER	**1 Tbsp. PARMESAN CHEESE,**
1 clove GARLIC, minced	**grated**

Cook broccoli to desired tenderness. While it is cooking, melt butter in a saucepan. Stir in garlic and almonds and cook over very low heat until almonds start to turn a golden brown. Stir in lemon juice, olives, and pimentos and cook a couple more minutes until everything is warmed through. Drain broccoli. Pour butter sauce over it; sprinkle with the Parmesan cheese and serve.

Serves 4.

Broccoli Souffle

Souffles are often intimidating to cooks. But they are well worth the effort—so go ahead and try it!

3 Tbsp. BUTTER
3 Tbsp. all-purpose FLOUR
1/2 tsp. SALT
1 cup MILK
1/4 tsp. ground NUTMEG
1 tsp. LEMON JUICE
1/2 tsp. ground BLACK PEPPER
dash CAYENNE PEPPER

1 1/4 cups BROCCOLI,
   cooked and finely chopped
   OR
1 package (10 oz.) cooked,
   chopped FROZEN BROCCOLI
4 EGG YOLKS
4 EGG WHITES

Melt butter in a saucepan; add flour and salt to make a roux. Slowly stir in milk and cook until it makes a white sauce. Stir in nutmeg, lemon juice, pepper, cayenne, and broccoli. Let mixture cool slightly. While it is cooling, beat egg yolks and then stir them into mixture. Continue to cool. Beat egg whites until stiff and gently fold into mixture. Pour into a lightly buttered 1 1/2-quart souffle dish or casserole dish. Bake in a 325° oven for 1 hour or until firm in the center. Serve with the following sauce.

Serves 4 - 6.

Broccoli Souffle Sauce

1/2 cup MAYONNAISE
1/2 cup SOUR CREAM

1 Tbsp. HORSERADISH
dash of CAYENNE PEPPER

Mix all of the ingredients together and serve with Broccoli Souffle.

Carrot Puff

2 Tbsp. PEANUT OIL	2 EGGS
1/2 ONION, chopped	1/4 tsp. HONEY
2 Tbsp. PARSLEY, chopped	1/4 tsp. ground GINGER
1 pound CARROTS, sliced	1/2 tsp. SALT
2 Tbsp. ORANGE JUICE	1/4 tsp. CAYENNE PEPPER

Saute onion and parsley in oil until just tender. Cook the carrots in enough water to cover for 10 minutes or until they are just tender. Let cool. Blend orange juice, egg, honey, and spices in a food processor or blender. Add the carrots and onion and parsley mixture, and blend again. Pour into a lightly greased casserole dish and bake in a 350° oven for 30 minutes.

Serves 4 - 6.

Chile Rice and Vegetables

2 Tbsp. OLIVE OIL	1 Tbsp. fresh PARSLEY, chopped
1 ONION, peeled and chopped	
1 CARROT, diced	1 tsp. CILANTRO, chopped
1 stalk CELERY, diced	2 tsp. ground RED CHILE POWDER
1 RED BELL PEPPER, seeded and diced	
1 cup uncooked BROWN RICE	1 tsp. ground BLACK PEPPER
2 cups CHICKEN BROTH	
1 cup WATER	1/2 tsp. SALT
1 TOMATO, peeled and chopped	

Pour olive oil into a 2-quart Dutch oven or heavy pan and heat for a couple of minutes over high heat. Put onion, carrot, celery, and bell pepper into pan; stir and turn heat down to medium. Cook for 5 minutes. Stir in rice. Add chicken broth, water, tomato, parsley, cilantro, chile powder, pepper, and salt. Cover and cook, over low heat, for 45 minutes or until the rice is done.

Serves 6 as a side dish.

Creamed Cabbage
with
Cheese

1 small head of CABBAGE
1 ONION, sliced
3 Tbsp. BUTTER
3 Tbsp. all-purpose FLOUR
1 cup MILK
1/2 cup grated CHEDDAR
    CHEESE

1/2 tsp. SALT
1/2 tsp. ground BLACK
    PEPPER
1/4 cup GREEN CHILE,
    chopped
1/4 tsp. CAYENNE PEPPER

Core cabbage and cut into sections. Boil onion and cabbage in lightly salted water until just tender. Drain and chop. Melt butter in a large frying pan. Whisk in flour to make a roux, then add the milk to make a white sauce (add more milk if necessary to make it the consistency you want.) Stir cabbage into white sauce. Add cheese, salt, black pepper, chile, and cayenne pepper. Cook over low heat for 10 to 15 minutes, stirring often, until cheese is melted.

Serves 6 - 8.

Eggnog Pancakes

Great served with Cranberry Sauce.

2 cups BISQUICK® BAKING MIX   1 1/2 cups EGGNOG
1 EGG

Put all ingredients into a bowl and beat until smooth. Heat a griddle, grease as you would for making any pancake. Pour batter onto griddle and bake until bubbles appear on top side. Turn and bake other side until golden brown.

Makes approx. 18.

Eggplant Casserole

In order to keep eggplant from turning black and bitter when preparing or cooking it, slice it, either peeled or unpeeled depending on what dish you're going to make, and place in a large bowl with 2 teaspoons salt and cover with cold water. Weigh down the eggplant with a plate to keep it under water. Let it sit at least 1/2 an hour. Drain it on paper towels. Place more towels on top, and again weigh down with plates.

2 large EGGPLANTS
1 pound ZUCCHINI
8 oz. CREAM CHEESE
2 EGGS, lightly beaten
1 tsp. CILANTRO, chopped
2 cloves GARLIC, diced
1/2 tsp. ground BLACK
    PEPPER

1/2 tsp. SALT
1/2 cup GREEN CHILE,
    chopped
1/2 cup seasoned BREAD
    CRUMBS
PAPRIKA
BUTTER

Peel eggplant and process according to the above directions. Cube eggplant and cook in lightly salted water until just tender. Peel zucchini and cut into cubes. Cook in a separate pan, in water, until just tender. Drain both of the vegetables and put into a lightly buttered casserole dish. Cut cream cheese into small cubes and add to the dish. Beat eggs and stir in along with cilantro, garlic, pepper, salt, and green chile. Top with bread crumbs; sprinkle with paprika, and dot with butter. Bake in a 350° oven for 30 minutes.

Serves 8.

Green Chile Grits Souffle

1 cup white corn GRITS
2 Tbsp. BUTTER
1 Tbsp. SUGAR
4 cups MILK
1/2 tsp. SALT

1/4 cup GREEN CHILE,
    chopped
2 EGG YOLKS, lightly beaten
2 EGG WHITES, stiffly beaten

Cook grits with butter, sugar, milk, and salt. When done, stir in green chile and egg yolks. Fold in egg whites and spoon into a lightly buttered baking dish. Dot with butter and bake in a 350° oven for 30 minutes or until lightly browned.

Serves 6 - 8.

Green Chile Rice

2 Tbsp. BUTTER
2 Tbsp. OLIVE OIL
2 cloves GARLIC, minced
4 GREEN ONIONS, chopped
1/2 cup GREEN CHILE,
    chopped

2 cups white RICE
4 cups CHICKEN BROTH
1 tsp. SALT
1 tsp. ground BLACK PEPPER

Melt butter in a saucepan. Add oil and saute garlic and green onions for 4 to 5 minutes. Stir in green chile and rice. Pour in chicken broth. Add salt and pepper. Cover and cook, over low heat, 20 minutes or until rice is fluffy.

Serves 4 - 6.

Holiday Cranberry Mold

1 lb. fresh CRANBERRIES
1 cup WHITE WINE
1 cup SUGAR
1 box (6 oz.) DARK CHERRY-
    FLAVORED GELATIN

2 cups BOILING WATER
1 cup COLD WATER
1 cup PECANS, chopped
2 tsp. ORANGE RIND, grated

Reserve a few cranberries to use as garnish. Run the rest of the cranberries through a blender or food processor to finely chop them. Boil cranberries, wine, and sugar in a saucepan for 5 minutes, stirring constantly.

Mix gelatin according to package directions using 2 cups of boiling water and ONLY 1 cup of cold water. Stir in cranberry mixture, pecans, and orange rind. Pour into a 3-quart mold. Chill in refrigerator for 4 hours or until set.

Unmold on a serving dish and garnish with the reserved cranberries and holiday greenery.

Serves 8 - 10.

Holiday Dressing

2 lbs. ITALIAN SAUSAGE
1 cup CELERY, chopped
1 cup ONIONS, chopped
1 lb. CHESTNUTS, boiled 10
    minutes, peeled and
    chopped
3 Tbsp. POULTRY SEASONING
1 pkg. (8 oz.) PREPARED
    STUFFING MIX

1 lb. BREAD CRUMBS
3 to 5 cups CORNBREAD,
    crumbled
3/4 to 1 cup WATER or
    CHICKEN STOCK
SALT and PEPPER to taste.

Remove sausage from casings, and fry until lightly browned. Remove from pan. Reserve and leave the fat in pan. Stir in celery and onions and cook until transparent. Drain, mix with sausage in a bowl, and add rest of ingredients.

Spoon into a lightly buttered Pyrex® baking dish and bake uncovered in a 325° oven for 1 hour or until lightly brown on top.

Serve with turkey, goose, or pork roast.

Holiday Quiche

This vegetable quiche makes a great addition to a buffet or as a vegetable course along with ham or turkey.

SHELL:

6 Tbsp. BUTTER
1 cup all-purpose FLOUR

1 tsp. grated ORANGE RIND
3 Tbsp. TEQUILA, chilled

Cut butter into flour. Add orange rind and tequila and work dough into a ball. Flour a board or piece of marble and roll out dough so that it will fit a 9-inch pie pan. Place dough in pie pan; line pie with aluminum foil, and fill with beans.*

Bake in a 350° oven for 10 minutes. Remove pie from oven and remove beans and foil. Fill with the following filling.

QUICHE FILLING:

2 Tbsp. BUTTER or MARGARINE
3 GREEN ONIONS, finely
chopped
1 RED BELL PEPPER, finely
chopped
1 cup BROCCOLI FLORETS,
cooked and chopped
3/4 cup SWISS CHEESE,
shredded

1/4 cup PARMESAN CHEESE,
grated
4 EGGS
1 cup MILK
1 Tbsp. DRY VERMOUTH
1/2 tsp. DIJON STYLE
MUSTARD
1/4 tsp. CAYENNE PEPPER

Melt butter in a frying pan and saute green onions and bell pepper until vegetables are limp. Spoon into pie shell. Spread broccoli over the other vegetables, and sprinkle cheese over them. Beat eggs, in blender, until frothy; then add milk, vermouth, mustard, and cayenne and blend. Pour over vegetables. Bake in a 350° oven for 35 to 40 minutes or until the center is set.

Serves 4 - 6.

*Beans are not an ingredient—just used to weigh down crust, if desired, so that it doesn't bubble up before putting in filling.

Holiday Squash

1 BUTTERNUT SQUASH	1/4 cup BROWN SUGAR
(approx. 2 1/2 to 3 lbs.)	1/2 tsp. grated NUTMEG
1/4 cup BUTTER or margarine	1/2 tsp. SALT
1 cup RAISINS	1/2 cup PIÑON NUTS
2 APPLES, finely chopped	

Cut squash in half. Scoop out seeds and add a small amount of water. Wrap with plastic wrap and cook in microwave until soft enough to scoop the squash out of the shell. Mash and mix the squash with the other ingredients. Spread out evenly in a lightly greased Pyrex® square baking dish. Bake in a 325° oven for about 20 minutes.

Serves 4 - 6.

Mashed Potatoes and Turnips

It seems that most every New Mexican took Scarlet O'Hara's dictum about never eating turnips again to heart. Here is a way to zip up your mashed potatoes for a holiday dinner and serve turnips to those folks who say they don't like 'em.

6 large POTATOES, peeled,	1/4 cup MILK
cut into quarters	1/2 tsp. ground BLACK
6 large TURNIPS peeled,	PEPPER
cut into quarters	1 tsp. SALT
1/4 lb. BUTTER	BUTTER

Boil potatoes and turnips separately in enough water to cover. Drain both and mash together with butter and milk (add more milk, if necessary). Stir in salt and pepper and serve hot with dots of butter.

Serves 6 - 8.

Onions Baked in Cream & Dill

4 cups ONIONS, sliced
1/2 tsp. SALT
1/4 tsp. ground WHITE PEPPER
1 tsp. PAPRIKA
1 tsp. DILL WEED, chopped

3/4 cup crushed SALTINE®
    CRACKERS
1 cup CREAM
2 Tbsp. BUTTER

Toss onions, salt, pepper, dill, paprika, and 1/2 cup of cracker crumbs in a casserole dish. Stir cream into the mixture. Sprinkle with the remaining cracker crumbs. Dot butter on top and bake in a 350° oven for 1 hour or until the onions are tender.

Serves 6.

Orange Pecan Sweet Potatoes

8 medium-size SWEET
    POTATOES, peeled
    and sliced
1 tsp. SALT
2 ORANGES, peeled and
    sectioned
1/2 cup BROWN SUGAR

1/2 tsp. SALT
2 Tbsp. ORANGE PEEL, grated
1/4 cup BUTTER, melted
1 cup ORANGE JUICE
2 Tbsp. ORANGE-FLAVORED
    LIQUEUR
1/2 cup PECANS, chopped

Place sweet potatoes in pan. Add enough water to cover and 1 teaspoon salt. Boil until just tender. Drain and spoon into a lightly buttered baking dish; top with orange sections. Mix remaining ingredients together, except pecans, and pour over oranges and sweet potatoes. Top with pecans and bake in a 325° oven for 30 minutes.

Serves 8 - 10.

Red Chile Potatoes

2 Tbsp. BUTTER
2 Tbsp. OLIVE OIL
2 cloves GARLIC, minced
1 large ONION, finely chopped
1 Tbsp. PARSLEY, chopped

6 POTATOES, peeled
   and diced
1/2 tsp. SALT
1 tsp. ground BLACK PEPPER
1 tsp. RED CHILE POWDER

Melt butter in a frying pan. Add olive oil and saute garlic, onion, and parsley for 2 to 3 minutes. Add potatoes, salt, pepper, and chile powder. Saute; cover and cook for 20 to 30 minutes or until potatoes are done.

Serves 4 - 6.

Scalloped Onions

It was July; it was hot, and we were finishing up this book. A friend sat across from my desk and said, "You've got scalloped onions in this book haven't you? I mean, it wouldn't be Christmas without scalloped onions!"

So here are scalloped onions!

4 cups PEARL ONIONS
4 Tbsp. BUTTER
4 Tbsp. all-purpose FLOUR
2 cups MILK
1/2 tsp. SALT
1/4 tsp. PAPRIKA
1 tsp. DRY MUSTARD

1/4 tsp. GARLIC POWDER
1/2 cup GREEN CHILE,
   chopped
1/2 cup CHEDDAR CHEESE,
   grated
BREAD CRUMBS

Cook onions in boiling water until they are just tender, and drain. Make a roux with butter and flour; stir in milk and make a white sauce. Stir in seasonings, onions, and chile and pour mixture into a lightly buttered baking dish.

Sprinkle the top with cheese and bread crumbs. Bake in a 350 ° oven for 30 minutes or until bubbly and light brown on top.

Serves 6 - 8.

Scalloped Oysters

1/2 box of SALTINE® CRACKERS (8 oz.), crushed
2 (8 oz.) cans OYSTERS, reserve juice

1/2 cup (or more) MILK
1 Tbsp. PARSLEY, chopped
1/2 tsp. CAYENNE PEPPER
1/4 lb. BUTTER or MARGARINE

Line the bottom of a square 2-quart Pyrex® dish with crushed crackers. Then a layer of drained oysters, then another layer of crackers, doing this until you end with a layer of cracker crumbs.

In a saucepan, heat the oyster liquid, milk, parsley, cayenne, and butter until the butter is melted. Pour this over the oysters and crackers. If there is not enough liquid to cover the crackers, add more milk.

Cook in a 350° oven for 30 minutes or until the liquid bubbles and top is slightly browned.

Serves 4 - 6.

Squash and Green Chile Molds

3 Tbsp. BUTTER
1/3 cup BREAD CRUMBS
1 cup CREAM or MILK
1/2 tsp. SALT
**1/2 tsp. ground BLACK
    PEPPER**
1/2 tsp. GARLIC POWDER

1/2 tsp. ground CUMIN
3 EGG YOLKS
**1 1/2 cups YELLOW SQUASH,
    cooked and chopped**
**1/2 cup GREEN CHILE,
    chopped**
3 EGG WHITES

Melt butter in a large saucepan and lightly brown bread crumbs. Add cream, salt, pepper, garlic powder, and cumin and cook over low heat, stirring constantly until mixture is smooth. Take pan off heat and let mixture cool slightly. Beat egg yolks and add cream mixture, a little at a time, beating constantly. Put mixture back into saucepan and cook for 3 to 4 minutes, stirring well. Remove from heat and stir in the squash and chile.

Beat egg whites until stiff and fold into the mixture. Put into 6 lightly buttered molds or custard dishes. Set them in a pan of hot water and bake in a 325° oven for 30 minutes or until set. Remove from oven and turn out on to serving plates to serve.

Serves 6.

Sweet Potato Souffle

Guylyn comes from a southern family — like many New Mexicans — and one of the things she insists on having for Christmas dinner is sweet potatoes. Here is a sweet potato dish that brings a different taste and appearance to a holiday table. It also gets rid of those ubiquitous, teeny, tiny marshmallows so many people put on top of their sweet potatoes.

2 cups cooked, MASHED SWEET POTATOES
1 cup SOUR CREAM
1/4 cup BRANDY
4 Tbsp. BUTTER
1/4 tsp. CAYENNE PEPPER
1/4 tsp. grated NUTMEG

1/2 tsp. SALT
1 Tbsp. LEMON RIND, finely grated
4 EGG YOLKS
6 EGG WHITES
1/2 tsp. CREAM OF TARTAR

Mix together sweet potatoes, sour cream, and brandy. Melt butter and stir into mixture. Beat until smooth. Stir in pepper, nutmeg, salt, and lemon rind. Beat egg yolks and stir into mixture. Beat egg whites almost stiff. Add cream of tartar and beat until very stiff. Fold egg whites into mixture and carefuly pour into a lightly buttered souffle dish. Bake in a 400° oven for 30 minutes or until done.

Serves 6 - 8.

Chapter Seven

Christmas in the Pueblos

Although many Indians now live outside the pueblos, they often try to return to their pueblo for Christmas. Who would want to miss the wonderful feasts and pageants held in the pueblos all through the holiday season?

Every pueblo celebrates Christmas with a unique blend of rites from ancient times and their own interpretation of the Christian holy days learned from the Franciscans. The dancers of the San Felipe Pueblo are dressed in masks and headdresses with real antlers and feathers. At the Acoma Pueblo, small clay figures of sheep and horses are left at the church. In the San Idlefonso Pueblo, Tasviyo has evolved into the Indian version of Santa Claus.

Most pueblos have in common the Matachine dancers, arrayed in their wonderful bright capes with streaming ribbons. These dances come from Mexico via medieval Spain like so many other New Mexican Christmas customs.

These elaborate dances that suggest hints of Moorish origins are usually led by a dancer wrapped in a blanket and carrying a large cross.

Each pueblo seems to have a different version of the dance. In Taos, a tall pole, reminding one of a May pole, is the focal point of the dance. The dancers wind and unwind long ribbons attached to the top of the pole.

During some years in the Taos Pueblo, instead of the Matachine dance, the dancers appear with deer antlers on their heads and carrying a stick in each hand representing the front legs of a deer.

In the San Juan Pueblo, the dance is performed both on Christmas Eve and on Christmas morning. A dance troupe is always comprised of 10 people. A guitar player and a man with nimble fingers on a well-worn fiddle furnish the music.

Two of the dancers sport clown-like outfits, and a young girl wearing a traditional white communion dress plays Malinche.

named after Cortez's Indian interpreter. She symbolizes chastity. A small boy portrays Toro in a buffalo headdress complete with horns. The Toro represents passion and brutality in counterpoint to the virtue and goodness of Malinche.

On the day after Christmas, the San Juan Pueblo enacts a turtle dance. Two mysterious figures with masks perform this sacred dance of the winter solstice.

Visitors to the Santa Clara Pueblo are treated to music played with guitar, fiddle, and drums, and the air is filled with the sounds of the songs of the pueblo.

At Santa Domingo Pueblo, the dances are performed for four days. And at San Ildefonso, Jemez, and Tesuque, one can also see the Buffalo Dance. The dancers with their leggings, decorated costumes, and the huge buffalo heads on their own heads are an impressive sight.

If one has grown up with the Hollywood version of Christmas including sleigh bells, trips to Grandma's house over covered bridges, snow-topped trees, and the only person in costume is Santa Claus—seeing Indians celebrate the Christmas season with a combination of ancient dances and Christian concepts can indeed be a very different experience and one that you will never forget.

It Is Christmas

The feathers cascading down their backs,
Moving in rhythm to the voices of
Their ancestors, augmented by drums
Of taut animal skins
The men danced through the pueblo
Seemingly oblivious to the Bermuda shorts
And flowered shirts of tourists
Whispering to each other "How cute!"

The smell of horno bread whets
Our appetites while wishing
The camera didn't have to be
Orphaned in the trunk
But rules are rules,
And Aunt E painted the pueblo
In 1925 anyway.

Wondering where Santa and candlelit
Church services celebrating Christ's birth
Fit into the undulating line of dancers
Under a hot December sun?
Where went the snow and sleigh bells
Of Currier and Ives?

Where is the babe in the manger,
And Mary and Joseph and those
Wise Men come from afar?

They are here!
Dressed in buckskin and beads
They are here,
And it is Christmas!

Cakes and Pies

Applesauce Cake

This is an old-fashioned cake that my grandmother used to make. It's great with a hot cup of tea after shopping for all those Christmas gifts!

1 3/4 cups CAKE FLOUR	1/4 lb. BUTTER
1 tsp. BAKING SODA	1 cup SUGAR
1 tsp. ground CINNAMON	2 EGGS
1/2 tsp. ground CLOVES	1 cup APPLESAUCE
1/2 tsp. ground NUTMEG	1 cup seedless RAISINS
1/2 tsp. SALT	POWDERED SUGAR

Sift flour with baking soda, spices, and salt. Cream butter into sugar. Beat eggs into sugar mixture; then stir in applesauce. Gradually add flour mixture, and beat until well blended. Stir in raisins. Pour into a well-greased 8-inch square cake pan, and bake for 45 minutes in a 350° oven or until cake tests done. Let cool. Sprinkle top of cake with powdered sugar.

TIP: *Place a paper doily on top of cake, then lightly sprinkle powdered sugar over the doily; remove doily, and you have an attractive, festive design.*

Cake de Frutas

(Fruit Cake)

This is a very simple, light fruit cake—easy to make and delicious.

1 tsp. BAKING SODA
1 cup WATER
1/3 cup BUTTER
1 cup SUGAR
1 EGG, lightly beaten
2 1/2 cups all-purpose FLOUR
1 APPLE, peeled and chopped
1/2 cup PECANS, chopped
1 cup GOLDEN RAISINS
1/2 cup candied ORANGE PEEL

1/4 cup candied LEMON PEEL
1 tsp. ALLSPICE
1 tsp. CINNAMON
1/2 tsp. GINGER
1/2 tsp. ground CLOVES
1/2 tsp. MACE
1/2 tsp. ground NUTMEG
1/2 cup LIGHT RUM

Mix baking soda and water together. Whip butter into sugar, then beat in egg. Stir soda water into sugar mixture. Stir in flour, apple, pecans, raisins, citrus peel, and spices. Spoon batter into a lightly buttered and floured loaf pan and bake in a 325° oven for 1 hour or until tests done. Remove from oven and let cool on a wire rack for an hour. Turn out onto rack and let cool totally. Pour rum over cake, wrap in wax paper and aluminum foil and store in the refrigerator, adding more rum occasionally if desired, until ready to serve.

Chocolate Orange Fudge Cake

4 oz. UNSWEETENED
    CHOCOLATE
2 cups CAKE FLOUR
2 tsp. BAKING POWDER
1/2 tsp. BAKING SODA
1/2 tsp. SALT
1/4 lb. BUTTER

2 cups LIGHT BROWN
    SUGAR
3 EGGS
1 tsp. VANILLA
1 cup MILK
2 Tbsp. ORANGE JUICE
1 Tbsp. ORANGE RIND, grated

Melt chocolate and let cool. Sift cake flour, then sift again with baking powder, baking soda, and salt. Cream together butter and brown sugar. Add eggs and beat well. Add vanilla, cooled chocolate, milk, orange juice, and orange rind. Stir in dry ingredients. Pour batter in two lightly greased and floured 8-inch layer-cake pans.

Bake at 350° for 30 minutes or until tests done. Cool on a wire rack; turn out and cool before frosting. Frost with Orange Delight Frosting.

Orange Delight Frosting

1/2 cup BUTTER or
    MARGARINE, at room
    temperature
1/2 tsp. VANILLA

1 lb. POWDERED SUGAR
2 Tbsp. ORANGE JUICE
1 Tbsp. ORANGE RIND, grated

Mix all ingredients together, adding more orange juice if necessary to make a spreadable consistency. Frost the cooled cake.

Christmas Coffee Cake

1/4 pound BUTTER	**2 cups all-purpose FLOUR**
1 cup SUGAR	**2 tsp. BAKING POWDER**
2 EGGS, lightly beaten	**1/2 tsp. BAKING SODA**
1 tsp. VANILLA	**1/8 tsp. SALT**
1 Tbsp. AMARETTO	**1/2 cup PECANS, chopped**
(almond-flavored liqueur)	**1/2 cup BROWN SUGAR**
1 cup SOUR CREAM	**3 tsp. ground CINNAMON**

Cream together butter and sugar. Add eggs, vanilla, amaretto, and sour cream and stir into the mixture. Sift flour with baking powder, baking soda and salt; combine with butter and egg mixture and beat until smooth. Pour half of batter into a lightly buttered and floured baking dish.

Mix together pecans, sugar, and cinnamon and sprinkle on top of batter. Pour rest of batter over pecans and bake in a 350 ° oven for 35 to 40 minutes or until done.

English Christmas Cake

This recipe was given to us by our good friend, Blanche Nelson Goldsmith. It originated in New England, and her grandmother was making this cake as early as 1900.

1 3/4 cups CANDIED CHERRIES, coarsely chopped
1 3/4 cups CANDIED PINEAPPLE, coarsely chopped
3 cups PECANS, broken
1/4 cup plus 2 Tbsp. BRANDY
1 cup BUTTER

2 1/4 cups SUGAR
6 EGGS, lightly beaten
4 cups sifted all-purpose FLOUR
1 1/2 tsp. SALT
1/2 tsp. BAKING POWDER
1 1/2 tsp. CINNAMON
1 tsp. ground NUTMEG

Line a 10-inch tube pan with aluminum foil. Mix the fruits, nuts, and 1/4 cup of brandy together and let stand while assembling the rest of the ingredients. Cream butter and sugar and beat until light and fluffy. Mix in eggs and beat well. Sift flour with remaining dry ingredients, then divide in half.

Stir half the flour into egg mixture along with 2 tablespoons of brandy. Stir other half of flour into fruit and nut mixture and coat them well. Then combine the two mixtures. Pour batter into a tube pan. Place a pan of water in the bottom of oven to keep cake moist, and bake for 3 hours and 45 minutes in a 275° oven or until cake tests done.

Remove cake from oven and let cool for 5 minutes, then remove from pan and let cool completely. Soak cheesecloth with brandy and wrap cake in it. Place in an airtight container or wrap with aluminum foil. Let stand 10 days then moisten cloth with more brandy.

Gingerbread Cupcakes

1/3 cup SOLID VEGETABLE
   SHORTENING
1/2 cup SUGAR
1/2 cup HONEY
1 EGG, well beaten
2 cups all-purpose FLOUR

2 tsp. BAKING POWDER
1/2 tsp. BAKING SODA
2 tsp. ground GINGER
1 tsp. ground CINNAMON
1 cup BUTTERMILK
1/2 tsp. SALT

Cream shortening with sugar and honey. Add egg and mix. Mix in dry ingredients alternately with milk and beat until blended. Place paper liners in muffin tins, pour 3/4ths full with the batter and bake in a 350° oven for 40 minutes.

Yield: approx. 16 cupcakes.

Gloria Blackstock's Kahlua Cake

Gloria, a good friend of ours, gave us this recipe. While she was talking about it, she told me that sometimes she adds a little more Kahlua than she wrote down in the recipe. A little more just makes it a whole lot better is her philosophy. I can attest that it is a sure-fire hit every time it's served and makes a nice dessert for a buffet or a wonderful gift.

Preheat oven to 325°

CAKE:

1 cup PECANS, chopped
1 pkg. (18 1/2 oz.) CHOCOLATE
    CAKE MIX
1 pkg. (3 3/4 oz.) INSTANT
    VANILLA PUDDING AND
    PIE FILLING MIX

4 EGGS
1/2 cup COLD WATER
1/2 cup OIL
1/2 cup KAHLUA®

Grease and flour a 10-inch tube pan or a 12-inch bundt pan. Sprinkle pecans over bottom of pan. Mix cake mix, pudding mix, eggs, water, oil, and Kahlua together. Pour batter over the pecans. Bake for 1 hour or until done. Let cool; then invert on a serving plate. Prick the top with a toothpick and evenly spoon and brush the following glaze over top and sides. Allow cake to absorb the glaze and repeat until all the glaze is used up.

GLAZE:

1/4 pound BUTTER
1/2 cup WATER

1 cup SUGAR
1/2 cup KAHLUA

Melt butter in a saucepan. Stir in water and sugar. Boil for 5 minutes, stirring constantly. Remove from heat, and stir in Kahlua.

Lady Baltimore Cake

The W. E. Gean family came to New Mexico in 1924. Of the five Gean children, one of them, Macon, was born on Christmas Day. His mother and, later, his sister, Lyndell Gean Morris, always made this cake for him on his birthday.

1/2 cup SOLID VEGETABLE SHORTENING	2 tsp. BAKING POWDER
	1/2 tsp. SALT
1 1/2 cups SUGAR	1 cup MILK
2 1/2 cups all-purpose FLOUR, sifted	1 tsp. ALMOND EXTRACT
	4 EGG WHITES, stiffly beaten

Cream together shortening and sugar. Sift flour, baking powder, and salt together. Stir in milk and almond extract; then combine with the sugar mixture. Fold in egg whites and pour into two greased and lightly floured 9-inch square cake pans. Bake in a 350° oven for 30 minutes or until cake tests done. Let cool. Make the following filling.

FILLING:

1 cup FIGS, chopped	1/2 cup RAISINS, chopped
1/2 cup PECANS, chopped	1/2 cup COCONUT, shredded

Mix together and stir in enough of the following frosting to make an easy-to-spread filling.

FROSTING:

2 EGG WHITES	1 tsp. VANILLA
1 1/2 cups SUGAR	COCONUT, shredded, for
5 Tbsp. COLD WATER	sprinkling on finished
1 1/2 tsp. LIGHT CORN SYRUP	cake.

Put all of the ingredients, except vanilla, together in the top of a double boiler. Cook, over boiling water, beating constantly with a portable mixer for 7 minutes. Remove from the heat. Stir in the vanilla and continue beating the frosting until light and fluffy.

ASSEMBLING THE CAKE:

Spread the filling on top of one of the cake layers. Top with the other layer, and spread the frosting over the top and sides of the cake. Sprinkle with shredded coconut and serve.

Maw Maw's Chocolate Cake

JoAnn Stuart Zufelt Wimberly gave us the following recipe and the story that goes with it.

"The Austin Stuart family of Artesia, New Mexico, had 10 children. All of them graduated from the Artesia High School beginning in 1928. In World War II, they were called 'the fighting Stuarts' because of their service in the armed forces.

Maw Maw, matriarch of the family, served this mashed potato cake at Christmas. With marriages and children, the family grew so large that there were usually 25 people at the huge table in the kitchen. They sat on benches instead of chairs, since there were so many of them."

3/4 cup BUTTER	**1/2 tsp. ground CLOVES**
2 cups SUGAR	**2 tsp. ground NUTMEG**
4 EGGS	**2 tsp. ground ALLSPICE**
1 cup MILK	**3 tsp. CINNAMON**
4 squares of UNSWEETENED	**3 cups all-purpose FLOUR**
CHOCOLATE, melted	**1 cup WALNUTS, chopped**
1 cup MASHED POTATOES	**1 cup PECANS, chopped**
1/2 tsp. SALT	**1 Tbsp. VANILLA**
4 tsp. BAKING POWDER	

Cream butter, sugar, and eggs together. Add milk, melted chocolate, and mashed potatoes. Add salt, baking powder, spices, and flour and stir well. Mix in the nuts and vanilla. Pour into four 9-inch lightly buttered and floured cake pans. Bake in a 350° oven for 45 minutes or until cake tests done.

ICING:

4 squares UNSWEETENED	**1/2 cup MILK**
CHOCOLATE	**1 tsp. VANILLA**
1 1/2 cups SUGAR	

Combine ingredients in a saucepan and cook until it comes to a soft ball stage. Beat until smooth. Ice each layer and top of cake.

Mincemeat Cake

2 EGGS	**1 Tbsp. BAKING POWDER**
1 cup SUGAR	**1/2 tsp. SALT**
1/2 cup BUTTER or	**1 tsp. VANILLA**
MARGARINE	**1 cup RAISINS**
2 cups MINCEMEAT	**1 cup PECANS, chopped**
2 cups all-purpose FLOUR	

Beat eggs and sugar together. Melt butter and beat into mixture. Add mincemeat. Sift flour, baking powder, and salt together in another bowl. Stir into mincemeat mixture and blend well. Stir in vanilla, raisins, and pecans. Put into a well-buttered 8-inch tube pan. Bake in a 350° oven for one hour or until cake tests done. Cool for 15 minutes then turn out onto a cake rack. Great with Bourbon Sauce below.

Bourbon Sauce

1/4 lb. BUTTER or	**2 Tbsp. COLD WATER**
MARGARINE	**2 Tbsp. BOURBON**
1 cup SUGAR or FRUCTOSE	**1/2 tsp. ground CINNAMON**
2 tsp. CORNSTARCH	**1/4 tsp. SALT**

Melt margarine in saucepan; add sugar and stir until dissolved. Stir cornstarch into cold water until dissolved then add to saucepan along with bourbon, cinnamon, and salt. Cook over low heat, stirring constantly, until sauce has thickened. Store in refrigerator.

Pumpkin Cake

We buy pumpkins every October to use as decoration for Hallow-een and Thanksgiving. Then, being somewhat frugal, we have to come up with ways to eat them. Here's one that does beautifully as a Christmas cake. It's especially nice when you're tired of making pies.

4 EGGS, lightly beaten
2 cups SUGAR
1 cup VEGETABLE OIL
2 cups all-purpose FLOUR
1 tsp. BAKING SODA
2 tsp. BAKING POWDER

1 tsp. ground CINNAMON
1 tsp. grated NUTMEG
1/2 tsp. SALT
1 cup PUMPKIN, cooked
       and mashed

Mix eggs with sugar and oil. Sift flour, baking soda, and baking powder together and add to egg mixture. Beat well; add spices and pumpkin. Stir and put into two lightly greased and floured 9-inch cake pans. Bake in a 300° oven for 45 minutes or until cake tests done. Cool on wire racks and then remove from pans. Ice cake with Cream Cheese Icing. Refrigerate until icing has set.

Cream Cheese Icing

8 oz. CREAM CHEESE, at
       room temperature
1/2 cup BUTTER, at room
       temperature
1 tsp. BRANDY (may
       substitute vanilla)

1 lb. POWDERED SUGAR
1/2 cup PECANS, chopped
MILK, if necessary

Blend cream cheese and butter together; then add the rest of ingredients and mix until smooth. Add milk to thin the mixture, if necessary. Ice top of each layer. Sprinkle with pecans and refrigerate.

Note: This cake must be KEPT refrigerated.

Pumpkin Pecan Cake

3 cups all-purpose FLOUR
2 tsp. BAKING POWDER
2 tsp. BAKING SODA
1 tsp. SALT
4 EGGS
2 cups SUGAR

1 1/2 cups VEGETABLE OIL
2 cups PUMPKIN, cooked and
    mashed
1 tsp. ground CINNAMON
1/2 tsp. ground NUTMEG
1 1/2 cups PECANS, chopped

Sift flour, baking powder, baking soda, and salt together. In mixing bowl, beat eggs, then gradually beat in sugar. Slowly add the oil and beat continuously. Blend in dry ingredients and pumpkin. Add cinnamon, nutmeg, and pecans. Pour into a bundt pan. Bake in a 350° oven for 1 hour or until cake tests done. Drizzle the warm cake with the following Praline Glaze.

Praline Glaze

2/3 cup light BROWN SUGAR
1/8 lb. BUTTER
1 Tbsp. EVAPORATED MILK

1/2 cup PECANS, chopped
1/4 cup BOURBON

Put sugar, butter, and milk in a saucepan and cook over medium heat until mixture starts to thicken. Remove from heat; add pecans and stir in bourbon. Pour over warm Pumpkin Pecan Cake.

Christmas Mince Pie

1 JAR (1 lb. 11 oz.) PREPARED
    MINCEMEAT
2 Tbsp. BRANDY

1 tsp. ORANGE RIND, grated
2 9-inch PIE SHELLS

Mix mincemeat, brandy, and orange rind together. Pour mixture into one pie shell; top with the second pie shell, and prick with the tines of a fork. Bake for 15 minutes in a 450 ° oven; then reduce the heat to 375° and bake for another 30 minutes or until pie crust is golden brown.

Christmas Pumpkin Pie

A lot of folks don't think Christmas dinner is complete without pumpkin pie, and I happen to be one of them. Here is a recipe we have used for several years.

2 EGGS, beaten
1 cup EVAPORATED MILK
2 Tbsp. melted BUTTER
1/2 tsp. ground CINNAMON
1/2 tsp. ground GINGER
1/4 tsp. ground ALLSPICE
1/4 tsp. ground NUTMEG
1/4 tsp. ground MACE
1 Tbsp. ORANGE PEEL, grated

2 EGGS
1/2 cup BROWN SUGAR
1/2 cup WHITE SUGAR
2 Tbsp. BOURBON
1 tsp. VANILLA
1/2 tsp. SALT
1 can (16 oz.) PUMPKIN
1 unbaked DEEP DISH PIE
    CRUST (9-inch)

Put all the ingredients, except the pumpkin, in a blender and blend until smooth. Place pumpkin in a bowl and beat the milk mixture into it. Pour into an unbaked 9-inch deep dish pie crust.

Bake for 15 minutes in a 400° oven. Reduce heat to 325° and bake for 30 minutes more or until the pie tests done. Serve plain or with whipped cream.

JoAnn Wimberly's
Rum Pecan Pie

JoAnn Wimberly nee Stuart is a fourth generation New Mexican who makes this wonderful pie for her family every Christmas Eve.

PASTRY:

1 cup all-purpose FLOUR
pinch SALT

6-8 Tbsp. cold BUTTER
3-5 Tbsp. cold BRANDY

Mix together all ingredients and chill in the refrigerator for 10 minutes. Roll out and put into a 9-inch pie tin. (Add more brandy if necessary to work the dough).

FILLING:

1/2 cup BUTTER, at room
  temperature
1/2 cup SUGAR
3/4 cup LIGHT CORN SYRUP
1/4 cup MAPLE-FLAVORED
  SYRUP

3 EGGS, lightly beaten
3 - 4 Tbsp. RUM
3/4 cup PECANS, chopped
3/4 cup PECAN HALVES

Mix butter, sugar, corn syrup, maple syrup, eggs, and rum together. Stir in chopped pecans and pour mixture into pastry shell. Top with pecan halves and bake 50 minutes to 1 hour in a 350° oven.

Maple Apple Pie

My father was a large producer of maple syrup during the years I was growing up in New York. One of the things the children looked forward to on Christmas Eve was having warm maple syrup to throw into the snow to make candy.

Since we have very little snow in southern New Mexico, I'm now content to import some maple syrup and make an apple pie with it.

2 9-inch PIE CRUSTS
6 cups sliced, peeled tart APPLES
1/2 cup MAPLE SYRUP
1/2 cup SUGAR
1/4 tsp. SALT

1 tsp. APPLE PIE SPICE
1 Tbsp. all-purpose FLOUR
1 Tbsp. LEMON JUICE
2 Tbsp. BUTTER
1 EGG, well beaten

Line a 9-inch pie tin with crust, and fill with apples. Mix maple syrup, sugar, salt, apple pie spice, flour, and lemon juice together. Pour over apples. Dot with butter, and cover with a top crust. Prick crust with tines of a fork, and brush with egg. Bake in a 450 ° oven for 10 minutes. Reduce heat to 350° and bake for 45 more minutes or until the top crust is golden brown.

Margarita Pie

1 Tbsp. UNFLAVORED GELATIN
1/2 cup LIME JUICE
1/2 cup TEQUILA
1/2 cup SUGAR
1/4 tsp. SALT
4 EGG YOLKS, lightly beaten

2 tsp. LIME PEEL, grated
3 Tbsp. ORANGE-FLAVORED LIQUEUR
1 9-inch PIE SHELL, baked
WHIPPED TOPPING

Dissolve gelatin in a little of the lime juice in a saucepan. Add tequila, remaining lime juice, sugar, and salt and cook, over low heat, until gelatin is dissolved. Add egg yolks and continue cooking until mixture starts to thicken. Remove from heat and stir in lime peel and orange liqueur.

Chill in refrigerator for 1/2 hour. Spoon into a baked pie shell. Top with whipped topping. Return to refrigerator and chill for an hour or until firm. Garnish with twisted lime peel.

Chapter Eight

Christmas in the City Different

From the first time I drove into Santa Fe, in the early sixties, down a narrow winding road past the centuries-old adobes, this city has captured my heart. The city different, as it calls itself, continues to delight me. My favorite time of year in Santa Fe is the Christmas season.

The Spaniards settled Santa Fe, naming it La Villa Real de La Santa Fe de San Francisco de Asis, after Saint Francis. Traditional custom relates that Saint Francis conceived the idea of commemorating the birth of Christ with more than words and thoughts. He wanted the faithful to visualize the biblical events in Bethlehem. Following the scene in a Roman basilica, he created a living nativity which became a symbol to the generations that followed.

Nacimientos (nativities) are displayed in homes and churches throughout New Mexico during the Christmas season. However, there is a spiritual feeling that Santa Fe becomes a living creche. It strikes a pastoral chord with many people trying to explain Santa Fe's magic during the holiday season.

One senses that the closest thing to being in Bethlehem on Christmas Eve in this country is being in Santa Fe. On that long ago night, Mary and Joseph wound their way through the narrow streets searching for an inn. Images of that journey emerge as one walks through the winding streets bordered by centuries-old adobes, past primitive buildings and stables. It could be that night in Judaea almost 2,000 years ago.

The miraculous and mysterious spiral stairway of The Chapel of Loretto, famous for not having a center support and thus defying gravity, is garlanded with evergreens. Down the street in St. Francis Cathedral, one can find an elaborate nacimiento.

In this jewel of a city, one sees many portrayals of Saint Francis surrounded by numerous animals, especially our native burro and sheep.

Santa Fe, founded in the early sixteenth century, has been discovered more than once—most recently by the jet set and celebrities of all ilk. Despite outside influences, the city different always seems to remain just that and is at no time more different than during the Christmas season.

When examining old periodicals about customs and happenings in New Mexico during the Christmas season, we also discovered some interesting traditions for the New Year. The following article gives a wonderful glimpse of a by-gone era in territorial New Mexico.

Santa Fe New Mexican

Santa Fe, New Mexico   December 30, 1909

NEW YEAR CALLS

There is no social custom more delightful or founded on more solid principles of good fellowship and good will than that of extending New Year greetings by friendly calls. To express good wishes and hopes for health and prosperity during the year just begun is a most gracious act of kindly feelings and is worthy of high appreciation.

The custom of New Year calls when it was almost universal, gave the best opportunity possible and often the only one for a man to renew acquaintances with old friends to learn of changes in their families and circumstances, and to show a continued interest in their welfare. Unfortunately in the large cities, the visiting list grew so large that it became impossible to make the rounds in person and so gradually the good old custom degenerated into the sending of cards and finally was largely discontinued. But in smaller cities and villages there is every reason that it should be continued and increased. The man who cannot devote one day in the year to kindly greetings to his friends is not worthy of having any friends and the lady who is not glad graciously to receive such greetings deserves no calls throughout the year. There is no necessity for refreshments, all that is essential is kindly feeling and sincere good will. The New Mexican hopes that in Santa Fe the callers may be many and that they may find open doors. While announcements of being "at home" are not necessary, yet the New Mexican will cheerfully publish such as are received.

NATIVITY SCENE

From the Collection of Mrs. Blanche Nelson Goldsmith

Christmas Sweets

Almond Bark

1 pound WHITE CHOCOLATE
1 cup SEEDLESS RAISINS
1 cup whole or sliced ALMONDS

Break chocolate into pieces and put into a 2-quart microwave-safe bowl and cook, uncovered, on high until chocolate melts stirring twice during cooking time. Remove and stir in raisins and almonds. Pour mixture onto wax paper. Cool thoroughly, break into pieces.

Yield: 1 pound candy.

Chocolate Coconut Kisses

3 EGG WHITES
1 Tbsp. all-purpose FLOUR
1 1/2 cups POWDERED SUGAR
1/4 tsp. SALT

1 tsp. VANILLA
1/2 cup SHREDDED COCONUT
1 cup SEMI-SWEET CHOCOLATE CHIPS

Beat egg whites until they form stiff peaks. Mix flour, sugar, and salt together; then slowly sprinkle over egg whites, beating constantly. Stir in the vanilla, coconut, and chocolate chips. Drop by teaspoon onto a lightly greased cookie sheet. Bake for 10 minutes in a 450 oven.

Yield: approx. 3 dozen kisses.

Chocolate Fudge

What would Christmas be without some good homemade fudge?

2 cups SUGAR
2 squares UNSWEETENED
    CHOCOLATE
1 cup EVAPORATED MILK
2 Tbsp. WHITE CORN SYRUP

2 Tbsp. BUTTER or
    MARGARINE
1 tsp. VANILLA
1/2 tsp. SALT
1 cup PECANS, chopped

Combine sugar, chocolate, evaporated milk, and corn syrup in heavy saucepan over low heat, stirring constantly until it begins to boil. Cook to the soft ball stage (238°F.) Remove from heat and cool for about 10 minutes. Add butter, vanilla, and salt and beat until mixture loses its sheen. Add the pecans and continue to beat for about 2 minutes.

Working quickly, spread out in well-buttered square pan until smooth. Cool and cut into squares.

Yield: About 16 pieces.

Divinity

1 cup BOILING WATER
3/4 cup LIGHT KARO® SYRUP
3 cups SUGAR
1/8 tsp. SALT

2 EGG WHITES
1 cup PECANS, chopped
1 tsp. VANILLA

Combine water, Karo syrup, sugar, and salt and cook until it reaches the soft ball stage when dropped into cold water. Beat egg whites until stiff; then add 1/2 of the sugar mixture, a tablespoon at a time, beating constantly. Continue to cook remaining 1/2 of the mixture until it forms the crack stage at 270°. Pour into egg mixture and beat until mixture appears dull. Fold in pecans and vanilla and drop, a spoonful at a time, onto waxed paper.

Yield: approx. 3 dozen pieces.

Peanut Brittle

I don't know anybody who doesn't like peanut brittle. To me it ranks right at the top of the list when I think about things to make for Christmas. Gloria Blackstock makes the best peanut brittle we've ever come across.

1 cup WHITE CORN SYRUP	3/4 tsp. SALT
1 cup SUGAR	3 cups RAW PEANUTS
1 Tbsp. BUTTER	1 tsp. BAKING SODA

Combine syrup, sugar, butter, and salt and cook over medium heat in a BLACK IRON SKILLET (Mrs. Blackstock has found that nothing else will work), stirring occasionally, until sugar melts. Add peanuts and stir constantly until peanuts become light brown in color. Remove from heat and quickly stir in baking soda. Lightly butter a shallow pan (a pizza pan or cookie sheet works). Let pan sit in a warm place until the butter melts - this will make the candy smooth. Pour peanut brittle into pan. Spread thinly and let set until hard. When you can loosen the edge, turn the candy over. Let candy set again and then break up into pieces for serving or gifts.

Penuche

2 cups BROWN SUGAR	1 tsp. VANILLA
3/4 cup MILK	1 cup PECANS, chopped
2 Tbsp. BUTTER	

Place sugar and milk in a heavy saucepan and boil slowly until it reaches soft ball stage (238° F.), stirring constantly. Remove from heat and add remaining ingredients. Beat until creamy and pour into a shallow pan, well-greased with margarine. Cut into squares when firm.

Serves 4 - 6.

Pralines

We both have wonderful memories of pralines. Guylyn's mother and grandmother used to make them every Christmas. My mother had a flamboyant friend who ran a candy shop and used to give us pralines every Christmas with the admonition that HER pralines were so remarkable that she only gave them to my mother and the Queen of England. It certainly made us feel special!

2 cups SUGAR
1 can (5 oz.) EVAPORATED
**   MILK**

2 Tbsp. BUTTER
2 cups PECANS
1/2 tsp. SALT

Put sugar, milk, and butter in a saucepan and cook, over low heat, stirring constantly until sugar dissolves. Add pecans and salt. Spoon pralines onto wax paper, about 2 inches in diameter. Let cool, and store in an airtight container. (Best when individually wrapped in plastic wrap.)

Yield: approx. 24 pralines

Truffles

1/4 pound UNSALTED BUTTER
1 1/4 cups POWDERED SUGAR
3/4 cup COCOA

1 EGG
2 tsp. DARK RUM
CHOCOLATE SPRINKLES

Beat butter until it is light and creamy. Sift together sugar and cocoa and mix half of it with butter. Mix in egg and rum, then the rest of the cocoa mixture. Chill in the refrigerator for 2 hours. Form into small balls and roll in chocolate sprinkles and serve.

Yield: approx. 12 pieces.

Apricot Empanadas

CRUST:

Use your favorite pie crust recipe or buy ready-made crust. Roll out and cut into 3-inch circles. Fill each round with the following apricot filling.

FILLING:

**2 cups APRICOTS, cooked or
    canned and drained**
1 cup SUGAR

1 tsp. CINNAMON
1 tsp. grated ORANGE PEEL
1 EGG, lightly beaten

Put apricots in blender with sugar, cinnamon, and orange peel and blend until not quite smooth (you want some lumps of apricot showing.)

Put 2 teaspoons of apricot mixture on each circle of dough. Fold in half; press edges together and seal - using a fork to make a design around edges. Place on a cookie sheet. Brush with beaten egg and bake in a 350° oven for 15 minutes or until lightly browned.

Yield: approx. 8 empanadas.

Christmas Breads and Sweets

Biscochitos

Our good friend, Mrs. Blanche Nelson Goldsmith, a native New Mexican and co-founder of the Daughters of New Mexico, makes these delicious New Mexican cookies every Christmas. This recipe, given to Mrs. Goldsmith by her aunt, is one of the best we've ever tasted.

Preheat oven to 350°.

1 cup SUGAR	1 Tbsp. BAKING POWDER
1 lb. LARD*	1 Tbsp. ANISE SEED
2 EGGS	1/3 cup ORANGE JUICE
1 tsp. VINEGAR	2/3 cup SUGAR
6 cups all-purpose FLOUR	1 tsp. CINNAMON
1 tsp. SALT	

Cream 1 cup sugar and the lard in a large bowl until fluffy. Add eggs and vinegar; beat well. Add flour, salt, baking powder, and anise seed alternately with orange juice, mixing well after each addition.

Divide into 4 portions. Chill for 30 minutes. Roll and cut one portion at a time into small diamond-shaped cookies. Dip cookies into mixture of 2/3 cup of sugar and the cinnamon. Place on ungreased cookie sheet. Bake 10-12 minutes or until golden brown.

Yield: approx. 12 dozen.

*You must use lard for this recipe. We have found that any substitute does not work.

Bourbon Date Nut Squares

2 EGGS
1/2 cup SUGAR
2 tsp. ORANGE RIND, grated
1/4 cup all-purpose FLOUR
1/2 tsp. BAKING POWDER

1 cup PECANS, chopped
1 cup DATES, chopped
3 Tbsp. BOURBON
3/4 cup POWDERED SUGAR
2 Tbsp. CREAM

Beat eggs and stir in sugar and orange rind. Beat together until light in color. Sift together flour and baking powder and stir into egg mixture. Mix in pecans, dates, and 1 Tbsp. of bourbon. Put into a lightly buttered and floured 8-inch square pan. Bake in a 350° oven for 30 minutes or until it tests done. Mix together powdered sugar, cream, and the rest of the bourbon. Ice and cut into squares.

Yield: approx 1 dozen squares.

Bourbon Snaps

1/4 lb. BUTTER
1/2 cup SUGAR
1 cup all-purpose FLOUR
1/4 cup BOURBON

1/2 tsp. VANILLA
1/4 tsp. ground NUTMEG
1/4 tsp. MACE
pinch SALT

Cream butter and sugar together. Sift flour and stir into butter and sugar mixture. Add bourbon, vanilla, nutmeg, mace, and salt. Stir well. Chill in the refrigerator for 1 hour. Drop by teaspoon onto a cookie sheet, two inches apart. Bake in a 375° oven for 5 minutes or until done.

Yield: approx. 2 dozen.

Buñuelos
(Christmas Doughnuts)

A lot of cultures have special fried bread, fritters, or doughnuts served especially around the holiday season. This recipe originally comes from Mexico and is served in a lot of New Mexican homes during the Christmas season.

1 1/2 cups all-purpose FLOUR	**1 EGG, lightly beaten**
1 Tbsp. SUGAR	**1/4 cup WATER**
1 tsp. BAKING POWDER	**MELTED BUTTER**
1/2 tsp. SALT	**COOKING OIL**

Mix together flour, sugar, baking powder, salt, egg, and water. Lightly flour a board and knead dough until smooth. Brush with melted butter. Put into a bowl; cover, and let stand in a warm place for an hour. Divide dough into 6 pieces and roll out on a floured board until very thin. Slice into long rectangles and let stand approximately 5 minutes. Fry in hot oil until golden brown, turning once. Drain on paper towels and serve warm with sugar and cinnamon, honey, or chocolate sauce.

Makes approx. 2 dozen.

Cinnamon Crisps

Flour tortillas are more versatile than most people imagine. When deep fried and sprinkled with a sugar and cinnamon mixture, they make a delightful cookie or garnish for ice cream.

8 8-inch TORTILLAS
OIL for deep frying

1 cup SUGAR
1 1/2 tsp. ground CINNAMON

Cut tortillas into quarters and deep fry until golden brown in oil that is approximately 350°. Mix sugar and cinnamon together and pour into a small paper bag. Remove tortilla quarters from oil. Place them in the bag and lightly dust with the sugar mixture.

Serves 4 - 6.

Cookies de Guadalupe

There are several recipes for cookies served at this time of year called "Cookies de Guadalupe." This is the recipe we like best.

1 cup BUTTER
1/2 cup POWDERED SUGAR
1 tsp. VANILLA
2 1/4 cups all-purpose
    FLOUR, sifted

1/4 tsp. SALT
1 tsp. ORANGE PEEL, grated
POWDERED SUGAR
    for dusting the cookies

Cream butter with sugar and vanilla. Add flour, salt, and orange peel. Stir mixture until it forms a stiff dough. Roll into a ball and chill in refrigerator for at least 4 hours. Pinch off portions of dough and roll into balls, approximately one inch in diameter.

Place balls on a lightly greased cookie sheet. Bake for 10 to 15 minutes in a 375° oven. Remove cookies from oven and immediately shake in a paper bag with powdered sugar. Let cool on a wire rack. Dust cookies with more powdered sugar.

Yield: approx. 2 dozen.

Cranberry Tart

1 1/2 cups all-purpose FLOUR
1/2 cup SUGAR
1/2 tsp. BAKING POWDER
1/2 tsp. SALT
1/4 tsp. ground CINNAMON
1/4 tsp. ground NUTMEG
1/2 cup LIGHT BROWN SUGAR
1/2 cup BUTTER

1 EGG
1/2 cup blanched ALMONDS,
    finely chopped
2 cups jellied CRANBERRY
    SAUCE
1 Tbsp. BRANDY
1 Tbsp. grated ORANGE PEEL
POWDERED SUGAR

Mix together flour, sugar, baking powder, salt, cinnamon, and nutmeg. Mix brown sugar with butter. Cut butter mixture into flour mixture with a pastry cutter; then add the egg and almonds. Keep 1/2 cup of dough for the top and chill it. Press the rest of the dough into an 8-inch pie pan, but don't cover the rim of the pan. Mix brandy and orange peel with cranberry sauce and spoon into the crust. Roll out rest of dough and cut into 1/2-inch strips. Place on the top of the filling in a crisscross pattern. Seal against the side of the pan, but don't put onto the rim. Bake in a 375° oven for 35 minutes. Remove from oven; let cool then sprinkle with powdered sugar.

Serves 6.

Date Bars

1 cup all-purpose FLOUR
1 cup SUGAR
4 EGGS, lightly beaten
2 cups DATES, chopped

2 cups PECANS, chopped
1 tsp. VANILLA
POWDERED SUGAR

Mix all ingredients (except powdered sugar) together. Spoon batter into a lightly greased shallow baking dish and bake in a 350° oven for 30 minutes or until tests done. While still hot, cut into bars; dust with powdered sugar and let cool.

Yield approx. 12 Date Bars.

Holiday Honey Cookies

Nancy Riley has a keen interest in food coupled with an extensive background in home economics. She gave us this recipe for cookies that will be well received at any holiday gathering.

1 cup BUTTER or MARGARINE	2 tsp. BAKING POWDER
1 cup HONEY	2 tsp. ground GINGER
1 cup SUGAR	1/2 tsp. VANILLA
1 EGG	1 1/2 cups PECANS, coarsely
3 cups all-purpose FLOUR	chopped

Cream butter. Beat in honey and sugar. Beat in egg. Mix in flour, baking powder, and ginger. Stir in vanilla. Mix in nuts. Drop by teaspoonfuls on greased baking sheet and bake at 375° for 12 to 15 minutes.

Yield: approx. 3 dozen cookies.

Holy Cookies

This recipe was given to us by our friend Marcia Ersland. She says she calls them Holy Cookies because "you can see through them as God sees through us!"

1 cup SUGAR	1 cup all-purpose FLOUR,
1/4 lb. BUTTER	sifted
(No substitutions)	1 cup OLD-FASHIONED
1 EGG	OATMEAL
1 tsp. VANILLA	1 tsp. ground CINNAMON

Cream together sugar, butter, egg, and vanilla. Mix in flour, oatmeal, and cinnamon. Form into small balls (about the size of a hazelnut.) Place on a lightly greased cookie sheet; then press out very, very thin with your fingers. Bake 6 to 10 minutes in a 350° oven until lightly browned. When done, remove immediately from cookie sheet to cool.

Yield: 3 dozen cookies.

Jimminy Christmas Cookies

Our good friend Marjorie Day enlisted the help of her children, Johnny and Marianne when making these delightful cookies for the holidays. It's a fun way to make Christmas cookies. Use different types of cake mixes and experiment with various toppings.

1 pkg. (18.25 oz.) CAKE MIX*	2 Tbsp. WATER
1/8 lb. BUTTER or MARGARINE	Your choice of Chocolate
1 EGG, lightly beaten	Chips, Fruit, etc.*

Preheat oven to 375°

Mix all ingredients together thoroughly. Chill dough in refrigerator for 1/2 hour. Roll dough into balls approximately the size of walnuts. Place approximately 2 inches apart on an ungreased cookie sheet. Bake in a 375° oven for 10 minutes or until the cookies are lightly browned. Let cool until cookies become crisp.

Makes approx. 3 dozen cookies.

*Some of the combinations Mrs. Day recommends are:

      Spice Cake Mix with Candied Fruit
      Orange Cake Mix with Chocolate Chips
      Cherry Cake Mix with Chocolate Chips
      Yellow Cake Mix with Chocolate Chips
      Yellow Cake Mix with Chopped Pecans
      Chocolate Cake Mix with Chopped Pecans
      Double Chocolate Cake Mix with Chocolate Mint Chips
      Spice Cake Mix with Butterscotch Chips
      Pineapple Cake Mix with Coconut

Mincemeat Empanadas

CRUST:

Use your favorite pie crust recipe or buy crust. Roll out crust and cut into 3-inch circles. Fill each round with mincemeat filling.

FILLING:

2 cups prepared MINCEMEAT   **1 Tbsp. BRANDY or BOURBON**
1 tsp. grated ORANGE PEEL   **1 EGG, lightly beaten**

Mix mincemeat, orange peel, and brandy together. Place 2 teaspoons of the mixture on each circle of dough. Fold in half; press edges together and seal - using a fork to make a design around edges. Place on a cookie sheet. Brush with beaten egg and bake in a 350° oven for 15 minutes or until lightly browned.

Yield: 8 empanadas.

CANDLESTICK ANGEL
With Christmas Breads
and Empanadas

Pecan Bites

1/2 cup SOLID VEGETABLE SHORTENING	4 Tbsp. all-purpose FLOUR
	1/2 cup PECANS, chopped
1 cup LIGHT BROWN SUGAR	1/2 tsp. SALT
3 EGGS	1 tsp. VANILLA

Cream shortening and sugar together. Beat in eggs, one at a time. Mix in flour and blend mixture well. Add pecans, salt, and vanilla. Drop the mixture by teaspoon 5 inches apart onto a well-greased cookie sheet. Spread mixture out, very thin with back of a spoon. Bake in a 300° oven for 10 minutes or until done.

Yield: Approx. 35 Pecan Bites.

Chapter Nine

Christmas in the Duke City

Christmas in Albuquerque means visiting a city decked out in the glow of light from innumerable luminarias. Tour buses bring thousands of holiday visitors into Albuquerque to see this amazing sight. On Christmas Eve, tourists and hometown folks alike travel around the city enjoying one of the largest grouping of farolitos, or luminarias, in the world.

Old Town in Albuquerque, an historic center, is especially decked out for Christmas. Its centuries-old adobes are outlined with luminarias on balconies, rooftops, window sills, sidewalks, and streets.

Buildings and town squares are gaily festooned with decorations from swags of greenery to balloons and ristras (strings) of chile peppers.

Albuquerque is always a hospitable city and it welcomes visitors with open arms, inviting all to sample some superb New Mexico cuisine.

If past newspaper accounts are any indication, the populace of the Duke City has long enjoyed celebrating the Christmas season.

Here is a very flowery piece on Christmas which read in part:

Albuquerque Daily Citizen

Albuquerque, New Mexico   December 23, 1899

PEACE ON EARTH GOOD WILL TOWARD MEN

Again the tides that flow from time into eternity have borne to the world the blessed anniversary which marked the dawn of hope for humanity, the day when man saw the ultimate victory over death and the triumph of the immortal over the mortal.

However, that same paper in the same year didn't mention Christmas on its front page in the December 25th issue. Nonetheless merchants still had gift-giving ads in that issue including one clothing store that touted a line of Christmas ties that "will startle you."

The **Daily Citizen's** lead stories for Christmas Day concerned a congressional committee from Washington D.C., which was in Albuquerque to discuss the matter of statehood, and an article about the Boer War from Pretoria, South Africa.

Ten years earlier, the **Albuquerque Morning Democrat** carried an advertisement for foodstuffs that caught our attention.

Albuquerque Morning Democrat

Albuquerque, New Mexico   Saturday, December 24, 1889

FOR XMAS.

Opossums EACH 65 to 90c.
Squirrels, 2 for 35c.
Rabbits, 2 for 35c.

Turkeys	Geese
Ducks	Chickens
Fresh Fish	Bulk Oysters
Florida Shrimps	Goose Breasts

Deeriott Farm Sausage, direct from
the Deeriott farm in Massachusetts
Mammoth Queen Olives.
24 varieties Fancy Cheese.
Christmas Veal.
Excelsior Farm Sausage.
Christmas Mutton.
Imported Cervelet.
Imported Magdeburger Dills.
Blue Points in shell, Little Neck Clams
in shell and Atlantic Lobsters on
sale Saturday.

Christmas Beef.
Fancy Mackerel.
Fancy Hams and Bacon
Home Made Sausages.
Mutton Meat
Fancy Cod Fish
Roasting Pigs.
Spare Ribs
Pork Tenders
Hams

In 1899, **The Daily Citizen** of Albuquerque printed a large story in its December 16th issue telling readers what goods were available to make their holiday season more enjoyable and where they could be purchased.

We have excerpted just a few of the offerings.

The Daily Citizen

Albuquerque, New Mexico   December 16th, 1899

GOOD THINGS FOR THE HOLIDAYS
Where to Get Substantials and
Delicacies for This Happy Season

———

"ALL THE COMFORTS OF HOME"

The Citizen devotes considerable space to brief write-ups for the principal firms of the territorial metropolis, showing where the good things for holidays can be purchased, where to get the substantials and delicacies for Christmas and New Year's, where to go for "All the comforts of Home," and where to eat, drink and be merry.

The Candy Kitchen needs no introduction. It is as usual, overflowing with sweets, nuts, fruits and dainties, without a doubt one of the most popular places in town.

The Albuquerque Grocery company carries all that is necessary to make a fine holiday dinner. The firm makes a specialty of first class canned goods, and being run on a cash system its prices are of the lowest.

F. G. Pratt & Co. are one of the oldest grocery firms in Albuquerque, and their business one of the largest. Careful attention to the wants of their customers, with good judgment in the selection of their stock, enables them to satisfy and retain their patrons. In their store everything can be found that goes to fill the wants of the appetite. Personal attention given to all orders and prompt delivery a feature.

The Fish Market is a feature of the town. Messers. Lamb & Stone have succeeded in catering to the wants of the public in a manner that pleases. A mere mention of all the good things they have to sell would mean a column of print.

Baked Peach Halves

6 PEACH HALVES
1/4 cup CREAM SHERRY
6 tsp. CURRANT JELLY

Place peach halves in a baking dish. Brush cream sherry over each half. Put one teaspoon currant jelly in center of each half, and bake in a 375° oven for 10 to 15 minutes. Great accompaniment for roast meat.

Fiesta Bananas

1/2 cup all-purpose FLOUR
1 Tbsp. ORANGE PEEL, grated
4 ripe BANANAS, peeled and
      cut in half
1 EGG, lightly beaten

6 Tbsp. BUTTER
1/2 cup CURRANT JELLY
1/4 cup dark RUM
1/4 cup SLIVERED ALMONDS

Mix flour and orange peel together. Dip bananas in egg, then in flour, then egg again and refrigerate for 1 hour. Melt butter in a frying pan and saute bananas, turning at least once until golden brown. Remove bananas to a serving plate and keep warm. Stir jelly and rum into the pan and deglaze it. Cook until mixture is smooth. Pour over the bananas; top with almonds and serve.

Serves 4.

Fried Apples

We are always pleased when Arthur and Alice Moore can join us at our holiday meals. Alice always brings something to share with everybody, these fried apples were one year's offering.

1 1/2 lbs. firm APPLES   **1/4 cup BROWN SUGAR**
3 Tbsp. BUTTER   **1/4 tsp. SALT**
1/3 cup BOILING WATER

Wash and core apples. Leave peels on. Cut into 1/2-inch thick rings. Melt butter in a frying pan and saute apples in butter until nicely browned on both sides. Dissolve sugar and salt in boiling water; pour over apples and simmer for 10 minutes. Remove apple rings from pan with spatula. Great as an accompaniment to roast pork or fried chicken.

Serves 4 - 6.

Honey-Baked Apples

Although I grew up eating baked apples, I never had any as good as these. The combination of honey, orange juice, and pecans makes a baked apple something special.

4 large APPLES   **1/2 cup ORANGE JUICE**
1/4 cup PECANS, chopped   **1/4 tsp. ground CINNAMON**
1/2 cup HONEY   **1/4 tsp. ground NUTMEG**

Core apples and peel each halfway. Fill core with chopped pecans. Mix together honey, orange juice, and spices. Pour mixture over pecans and let it run over the sides of the apples.

Pour a 1/2-inch of hot water in a baking dish. Place apples in the water. Cover with aluminum foil and bake in a 350° oven for 45 minutes. Remove foil and bake for another 15 minutes or until done.

Serves 4.

Spiced Fruit Compote
with Almonds

2 large ripe BANANAS, sliced
2 RED APPLES, sliced
2 PEARS, sliced
1 cup SEEDLESS GREEN
    GRAPES, cut in half
2 ORANGES, peeled and
    sectioned

1 Tbsp. LEMON JUICE
1/4 cup HONEY
6 sprigs fresh MINT
1/4 tsp. ground NUTMEG
1/4 tsp. ground CINNAMON
1 cup ALMONDS, sliced

Put the fruit in a large serving bowl (glass works nicely). Sprinkle with lemon juice so that the fruit won't turn dark.

Put honey into a saucepan over low heat and stir in the mint, nutmeg, and cinnamon. Heat and stir until well-mixed. Let cool; then stir into bowl of fruit. Chill, sprinkle with sliced almonds and serve at once.

Serves 4 - 6.

Amaretto Rice Pudding

3 EGGS, lightly beaten
3/4 cup SUGAR
1/4 tsp. SALT
2 cups MILK
1 1/2 cups COOKED
    WHITE RICE

1/2 tsp. ground CINNAMON
1 tsp. ORANGE RIND, grated
1/4 cup AMARETTO
    (almond-flavored liqueur)
2 tsp. VANILLA
1/4 tsp. ground NUTMEG

Mix together eggs, sugar, and salt. Slowly beat in milk. Stir in rice, cinnamon, orange rind, amaretto, and vanilla. Pour mixture into a lightly greased 1 1/2 quart baking dish. Sprinkle nutmeg on top. Place dish in a larger pan with approximately 1 inch of water. Bake for 1 hour in a 325° degree oven or until nicely browned on top.

Serves 6 - 8.

Apple Raisin Pudding

3/4 cup RAISINS

1/4 cup BRANDY

2 cups BREAD CRUMBS

1 cup MILK

3 APPLES, peeled, cored and
   chopped

1/4 cup all-purpose FLOUR

1/2 tsp. ground CLOVES

1/2 tsp. ground NUTMEG

1/2 tsp. ground CINNAMON

3 EGGS, lightly beaten

Plump raisins in brandy for 1/2 hour. Mix bread crumbs with milk. Stir in rest of the ingredients; add raisins with brandy. Mix well and then spoon into a well-buttered baking dish and bake in a 375° oven for 45 minutes. Serve with whipped cream spiked with a little brandy.

Serves 4 - 6.

Christmas Plum Pudding

1/2 cup BUTTER	1/2 tsp. ground MACE
1 cup SUGAR	1 tsp. ground CINNAMON
3 EGGS, lightly beaten	1/2 tsp. ground CLOVES
2 cups MILK	2 Tbsp. ORANGE PEEL, grated
3 cups soft WHITE BREAD	1 Tbsp. LEMON PEEL, grated
CRUMBS	1 1/2 cups RAISINS
1 tsp. BAKING POWDER	1/4 cup CURRANTS
1 tsp. SALT	1/4 cup FIGS, chopped
1/2 tsp. ground NUTMEG	1/2 cup PECANS, chopped

Cream butter and sugar together. Mix eggs with milk and pour over the butter mixture. Add bread crumbs, baking powder, salt, spices and mix again. Add remaining ingredients and stir well. Butter a large (2-quart) mold and fill it 3/4 full with the batter. Cover tightly with aluminum foil. Set mold in a pan of hot water, half way up the sides of mold, and steam pudding in a 325 ° oven for 3 hours. Serve warm with Hard Sauce.

Serves 8 - 10.

Hard Sauce

1 cup POWDERED SUGAR
1/2 cup BUTTER, at room temperature
1 tsp. BRANDY or vanilla

Mix all the ingredients together and refrigerate at least 2 hours before serving.

Easy Christmas Trifle

DRY WHITE or YELLOW LAYER
CAKE, not iced
1 cup RASPBERRY JAM
6 Tbsp. RUM
6 Tbsp. DRY SHERRY
1/2 cup blanched slivered

ALMONDS
2 cups prepared VANILLA
PUDDING
1 cup whipping CREAM
2 tsp. SUGAR

In a large glass bowl, place a layer of cake spread with some of the jam. Sprinkle with 2 tablespoons of sherry and rum. Top with some of the almonds; spread some pudding on top of almonds. Repeat the procedure 2 times. Whip cream until it starts to form peaks. Add sugar and continue beating until cream forms stiff peaks. Spread on top of the trifle. Refrigerate for at least 2 hours and serve.

Serves 6 - 8.

New Mexican Bread Pudding

Preheat Oven to 350°.

2 EGGS, lightly beaten
2 cups MILK
1 Tbsp. VANILLA*
1/2 cup SUGAR
2 Tbsp. BROWN SUGAR
1 tsp. ground CINNAMON
1/2 tsp. ground NUTMEG

4 cups dry or stale BREAD,
   torn into pieces
1/2 cup SEEDLESS RAISINS
1/2 cup PECANS, chopped
1 cup MONTEREY JACK
   CHEESE, cubed

Beat eggs into milk and vanilla. Stir sugars, cinnamon, and nutmeg into the mixture. Pour mixture over bread and stir until absorbed. Stir in raisins, pecans, and cheese. Pour mixture into a greased baking dish. Bake in a 350° oven for 25 minutes. Serve with the following Kahlua Sauce.

Serves 6.

You read it right! 1 <u>tablespoon</u> of vanilla makes it GOOD!

Kahlua Sauce

2 Tbsp. BUTTER
2 Tbsp. All-purpose FLOUR
1 cup boiling WATER

2 Tbsp. BROWN SUGAR
1 tsp. VANILLA
2 Tbsp. KAHLUA®

Melt butter in a sauce pan. Stir flour into butter, and gradually add water, stirring constantly. Add sugar and vanilla. Simmer mixture over low heat until it bubbles. Remove from heat, and let mixture cool slightly. Add Kahlua; stir well. Serve warm over New Mexican Bread Pudding.

Chapter Ten

The Many Cultures
of a
New Mexican Christmas

Although the Indian and Mexican heritage of New Mexico comes instantly to mind when talking about Christmas in the Land of Enchantment—many other ethnic cultures have also played a significant role.

French immigrants settled in and around Mora, in the northern part of the state, bringing with them the love of good food and wine. Germans also brought their hearty food with them to the territory and then the state. Later, during World War II there were prisoner of war camps in the state, and there is a rumor that some of the Italian and German POW's "walked away," went underground, and became integrated into the population.

In the Thirties, people escaping the "dust bowl" got as far as New Mexico, either running out of money or stamina, and settled in the state, bringing with them a desire to work hard and the customs inherited from their European ancestors.

Over the years, men following the dream of "gold in them thar hills"; blacks escaping hard times in the South; folks called "Lungers" suffering from tuberculosis and looking for the climate that would cure them; families taking to heart the cry to go west; snow birds; and yuppies have all left their individual stamp on the way we do things.

All these people from other parts of the world and this country have given us a legacy that has made its mark on the customs and traditions of the state. This coupled with the Indian and Mexican influences make Christmas in New Mexico one of the most unique, satisfying, and unforgettable experiences possible.

Christmas Angel

St. Nicholas
One of a series of
handcrafted Santos
by David Dietrich

Acoma Pot - Circa 1925

Pueblo Indians with dried corn

Beverages

Cafe Tecolote

I was told by a wise old man (who claimed to be a descendant of one of Coronado's men and his Indian bride) that if you heard an owl (tecolote) hoot on Christmas Eve, you would get whatever you wished for.

4 tsp. MEXICAN CHOCOLATE*
4 oz. TEQUILA
    (I use the "gold" tequila
    for this recipe)

4 cups strong, HOT COFFEE
WHIPPED CREAM
NUTMEG

Put 1 teaspoon of chocolate in the bottom of each mug. Pour an ounce of tequila over it and muddle until the chocolate dissolves. Pour the coffee in the mug. Top with the whipped cream and sprinkle with nutmeg.

Serves 4.

*Available in many specialty stores or the ethnic sections of super-markets. If you can't find it, mix 3 1/2 tsp. cocoa with 1/2 tsp. cinnamon as a substitute.

Eggnog de Posada

(Rompope)

The cold and weary travelers who comprise a posada welcome all sorts of beverages to warm them. The more seasoned of the group may down a shot of straight tequila. But homemade wines; coffee with liqueur; hot chocolate and various punches, both alcoholic and non-alcoholic, are all extremely popular. This eggnog can either be a great start or dramatic finale to a posada.

6 EGG YOLKS
1/2 cup SUGAR or FRUCTOSE
1 Tbsp. VANILLA
1 quart MILK

2 oz. BANANA-FLAVORED
    LIQUEUR
2 oz. RUM
WHIPPED CREAM and NUTMEG

Beat egg yolks, sugar, and vanilla together in a bowl or blender until a light lemon yellow color. Add milk, banana liqueur, and rum. Pour into glasses. Top with a dollop of whipped cream and sprinkle with nutmeg.

Yield: approx. 1 quart.

Holiday Cranberry Cocktail

Makes 1 Drink

1 oz. RUM
1/2 cup CRANBERRY JUICE
1/4 tsp. LEMON JUICE

2 or 3 ICE CUBES
CLUB SODA

Blend everything, but club soda, in a blender. Pour into a tall glass, over ice. Fill with club soda; stir and serve.

Hot New Mexican Cider

1 gal. APPLE CIDER
1/4 cup LEMON JUICE
2 or 3 CINNAMON STICKS
1 1/2 cups TEQUILA

1/4 cup ORANGE-FLAVORED
LIQUEUR
thin LEMON and ORANGE
SLICES

Put apple cider, lemon juice, and cinnamon sticks in a large enamel pot and cook over low heat until hot. Pour tequila and orange liqueur into a punch bowl. Pour in cider mixture and stir. Float lemon and orange slices on top and serve.

Serves 12 - 18

Mulled Cider

We serve this mulled cider every Christmas and always make two versions—one with liquor and one without. Either way, it is a delicious drink to serve guests who drop by during a posada or for a more formal party.

**3 CINNAMON STICKS
broken in half
1 Tbsp. WHOLE CLOVES
1 tsp. ALLSPICE
1 tsp. NUTMEG
1 tsp. MACE**

**1/2 tsp. POWDERED GINGER
1 gallon APPLE CIDER
2 ORANGES, sliced with
seeds removed
2 LEMONS, sliced with
seeds removed**

Put all the spices in a spice bag or a clean cloth, such as cheese cloth, and tie securely. Place bag in a large pot. Pour cider over it and simmer for 30 minutes.

Remove spice bag and pour into a heavy silver or china punch bowl. Keep some cider on the stove, on very low heat, to add to the punch bowl as it is depleted and cools off. Add sliced fruit to bowl and serve.

Mulled Cider
with
ST. NICHOLAS' "STICK" IN IT

Guests exclaim how good this punch is and then ask for the recipe. When we give it to them, they can't believe that it has a combination of gin and bourbon in it. This came about because one of us enjoys bourbon and one of us enjoys gin, so we decided to try both. As unlikely as the combination is, it turned out to be not only delicious but a family stand-by.

1 cup GIN   And   2 cups BOURBON

Make the Mulled Cider recipe above. Pour gin and bourbon into a punch bowl. Then pour mulled cider over liquor and stir. Add the sliced fruit and serve.

New Mexican Hot Chocolate

This is a great warmer-upper for children and adults alike. The cinnamon and almonds make it truly unique.

4 cups MILK
2 CINNAMON STICKS, halved

Heat milk with the cinnamon sticks, over low heat, until milk is warm.

4 tsp. UNSWEETENED COCOA
8 tsp. BROWN SUGAR
WHIPPED CREAM
SLIVERED ALMONDS

Put one teaspoon of cocoa and two teaspoons of brown sugar in each mug. Pour cinnamon milk in and stir until cocoa and sugar are dissolved. Reserve cinnamon sticks. Top with whipped cream and slivered almonds. Place one cinnamon stick in each mug.

Serves 4.

Punch de Posada

1 can (46 oz.) PINEAPPLE JUICE
1 cup ORANGE-FLAVORED LIQUEUR
1 cup TEQUILA
1/4 cup BRANDY
1/4 cup LIME JUICE
1 liter CLUB SODA or 7-UP®

Mix all together. Pour over a block of ice* in a punch bowl.

Serves approx. 20.

*Fill a 2-quart mold with water. Add sliced limes and/or oranges and red maraschino cherries. Freeze until solid. Unmold into a punch bowl. Pour the punch over the ice.

Index

Feliz Navidad!

About the Author

Lynn Nusom has owned and operated award winning restaurants and was the executive chef of a four-star four-diamond hotel. He has written over 700 newspaper and magazine articles on food, reviews cookbooks, makes frequent appearances on television demonstrating cooking techniques and gives lectures on southwestern cuisine.

Lynn Nusom is the author of eight cook books: *The New Mexico Cook Book, The Tequila Cook Book, The Sizzling South-western Cookbook, Christmas in New Mexico, Christmas in Arizona, Cooking in the Land of Enchantment, Spoon Desserts; Custards, Cremes and Elegant Fruit Desserts,* and *The Billy-The-Kid Cookbook.*

The author makes his home in southern New Mexico with his wife, Guylyn Morris Nusom.

SALSA LOVERS COOK BOOK

More than 180 taste-tempting recipes for salsas that will make every meal a special event! Salsas for salads, appetizers, main dishes, and desserts! Put some salsa in your life! By Susan K. Bollin.

5 1/2 x 8 1/2—128 pages . . . $5.95

QUICK-N-EASY MEXICAN RECIPES

More than 175 favorite Mexican recipes you can prepare in less than thirty minutes. Traditional items such as tacos, tostadas and enchiladas. Also features easy recipes for salads, soups, breads, desserts and drinks. By Susan K. Bollin.

5 1/2 x 8 1/2—128 pages . . . $5.95

CHIP & DIP LOVERS COOK BOOK

More than 150 recipes for fun and festive dips. Make southwestern dips and dips with fruits , vegetables, meats, poultry and seafood. Salsa dips and dips for desserts. Includes recipes for making homemade chips. By Susan K. Bollin.

5 1/2 x 8 1/2—112 pages . $5.95

CHILI-LOVERS' COOK BOOK

Chili cookoff prize-winning recipes and regional favorites! The best of chili cookery, from mild to fiery, with and without beans. Plus a variety of taste-tempting foods made with chile peppers. 150,000 copies in print! By Al and Mildred Fischer.

5 1/2 x 8 1/2—128 pages . . . $5.95

WHOLLY FRIJOLES!
The Whole Bean Cook Book

Features a wide variety of recipes for salads, main dishes, side dishes and desserts with an emphasis on Southwestern style. Pinto, kidney, garbanzo, black, red and navy beans, you'll find recipes for these and many more! Includes cooking tips and fascinating bean trivia! By Shayne Fischer.

5 1/2 x 8 1/2—112 pages . . . $6.95

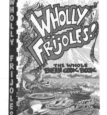

ORDER BLANK

GOLDEN WEST PUBLISHERS

☼ 4113 N. Longview Ave. • Phoenix, AZ 85014

602-265-4392 • **1-800-658-5830** • FAX 602-279-6901

Qty	Title	Price	Amount
	Apple Lovers Cook Book	6.95	
	Arizona Cook Book	5.95	
	Best Barbecue Recipes	5.95	
	Chili-Lovers' Cook Book	5.95	
	Chip and Dip Lovers Cook Book	5.95	
	Christmas in Arizona Cook Book	8.95	
	Christmas in Colorado Cook Book	8.95	
	Christmas in New Mexico Cook Book	8.95	
	Christmas in Texas Cook Book	8.95	
	Christmas in Washington Cook Book	8.95	
	Cowboy Cartoon Cook Book	5.95	
	Grand Canyon Cook Book	6.95	
	Joy of Muffins	5.95	
	New Mexico Cook Book	5.95	
	Quick-n-Easy Mexican Recipes	5.95	
	Salsa Lovers Cook Book	5.95	
	Tequila Cook Book	7.95	
	Texas Cook Book	5.95	
	Tortilla Lovers Cook Book	6.95	
	Wholly Frijoles! The Whole Bean Cook Book	6.95	
Shipping & Handling Add ➡	U.S. & Canada	$3.00	
	Other countries	$5.00	

☐ My Check or Money Order Enclosed $

☐ MasterCard   ☐ VISA ($20 credit card minimum)

(Payable in U.S. funds)

Acct. No.	Exp. Date
Signature	
Name	Telephone
Address	
City/State/Zip 8/97	**Call for FREE catalog** Xmas N. M.

This order blank may be photo-copied.